THE
Mindfulness
COOKBOOK

THE

Mindfulness
COOKBOOK

EAT IN THE 'NOW'
AND BE YOUR PERFECT
WEIGHT FOR LIFE

Dr Patrizia Collard & Helen Stephenson

hamlyn

An Hachette UK Company
www.hachette.co.uk

First published in Great Britain in 2015 by
Hamlyn, a division of Octopus Publishing Group Ltd
Endeavour House
189 Shaftesbury Avenue
London WC2H 8JY
www.octopusbooks.co.uk

ISBN 978 0 60063 169 9

A CIP catalogue record for this book is available from the
British Library

Printed and bound in China

10 9 8 7 6 5 4 3 2 1

Contents

Recipes

Features

Introduction

How often do we think about food, or the effect food has on our bodies? We are living in a culture that is obsessed with the young, the good-looking and the slim. Most of us, to a greater or lesser degree, are unhappy with the way we look and whether we relate that to our eating habits or not, we think about food many times during the day.

Definition of mindfulness

Mindfulness lies at the core of Buddhist meditative practices but it is universal. It can be described as a way of being, a way of seeing and a way of connecting to your senses.

> **'The present is the only time that any of us have to be alive, to know anything, to perceive, to learn, to act, to change, to heal.'**
>
> JON KABAT-ZINN

Staying in touch with the present in a mindful way from one moment to the next may lead to you experiencing life differently. You may become a little less stuck in your ways, perceiving more options and finding more strength, more balance, more understanding and confidence. The practice of mindfulness can diffuse our negativity, aggression and unstable emotions.

Mindfulness has also been described as 'bare attention'. That term was coined by German-born Buddhist monk N Thera, one of the great figures of 20th-century Buddhism. It is called 'bare' because it attends just to the bare facts of perception as presented, either through the five senses or through the mind, without reacting to them or judging them. We behave rather like an outside observer, perceiving what is happening to us, accepting and allowing it. The thoughts or feelings we observe are not us, they are just something that is happening to us.

The fusion of mindfulness-based stress reduction (MBSR) and mindfulness-based cognitive therapy (MBCT)

Research estimates that around 20 per cent of the population in Western countries will suffer an episode of clinical depression at least once in their lifetime. However, up until the 1990s, CBT (cognitive behavioural therapy) research did not explore the fact that patients who have had more than one or two episodes of depression are susceptible to becoming depressed again and again. Very little hard data focused on this phenomenon of 'relapse' until researchers began to look for a more cost- and time-effective intervention to deal with it. Regular CBT would be used for acute depression and the 'new approach' of MBSR would hopefully cater for relapse prevention.

HOW MBCT WORKS

- Identify your cognitive 'distortions' – conscious awareness.
- Identify the fact that the imagined 'threat' is only a thought.
- Sit with what 'is' – I am okay, even now.
- Appraise your internal resources – 'I can'.

Mindfulness-based cognitive therapy is an integration of mindfulness-based stress reduction with cognitive behavioural therapy. In conventional CBT, the focus is on changing unhelpful beliefs. In MBCT, the focus is rather on methodical training to be more aware, moment by moment, of physical sensations and of thoughts and feelings as mental events. Research on MBCT shows that it can halve the relapse rate in recovered patients who have had three or more episodes of depression. Other targeted versions of MBCT have now been developed, including MBCT for chronic-fatigue syndrome, for oncology patients, in schools, for anxiety disorders and in the treatment of trauma, to mention just a few. Mindfulness-based eating interventions are being developed as we speak.

What is mindful eating?

By bringing mindfulness into your life, more specifically into your eating life, you will learn to stop, to tune in and to listen. You will become interested in what is really important to you. Through the various practices in this book, you make time and pay attention to what is going on in your life right now. You will come to understand how your thoughts and feelings, if unnoticed, can pull you away from the present moment, and make you go for the chocolate to avoid the discomfort of feeling upset or lonely.

When we pay attention to our food intake, we have to face our true longings and explore what we really want. By not being mindful with our 'true' hunger, we tend to eat more, when having less could be what is needed. By becoming mindful we develop understanding, and in this process we become more forgiving and kinder to ourselves. Just by reading this book you can start to replace hating your body with appreciating your inner wisdom. You can release yourself from the grip of shame and anger and replace it with understanding. You will become less obsessed about food and how you look and more attuned to the appreciation of being alive.

Reading this book, and practising the exercises, will help you to:

- *reconnect* with your body and its senses

- *retrain* yourself to enjoy your food without guilt or shame

- *feel full* and eat less as you learn to feel truly nourished

- *break free* from destructive eating habits

- *become aware* of the feelings and thoughts that keep your unhelpful eating patterns in place

- *reconnect* with your own inner wisdom

- *live life* with zest and creativity

- *free yourself* from negative thinking and develop compassion and kindness.

Factors that influence our eating habits

The genetic code

'It is obvious that some people have a larger frame than others, but holding on to the idea that our weight is dictated solely by genetics assumes that change is impossible. Mindful eating invites us to accept the fact that we cannot change the basic frame of our bodies, but that we can still find our own ideal weight, together with a healthy sense of appreciation and respect for our bodies.

Reward and punishment

There are countless times when we have eaten something unhealthy (and delicious) because 'we are worth it'; and times when we have felt obliged to eat something that we don't like. We may assume it's normal to live with this inner struggle of 'I must' and 'I mustn't'. By becoming a witness to the feelings, a space is created around them and we are no longer a hostage to them.

The teenage years

Being a teenager is a time of constant changes in the body and a time when we become self-conscious about our size and eating habits. Views are formed about how we see ourselves and how others see us. But now it is important to acknowledge that whatever it was happened in the past. Mindfulness enables us to let go of those stories and feelings, and to replace them with what is needed now.

Emotions

Very few people in the West eat out of hunger alone. Most of us eat from a place of emotion. We often do things, such as eating chocolate while watching TV, without being conscious of the thoughts and feelings that drive the behaviour. We live and eat on autopilot, reacting to signals from the brain or cravings from the mind. Mindfulness is about having the awareness to see the formation of the emotion, to see its origins, and with practice, even to see the very first thought that started it all.

Lack of exercise

We live in a sedentary world. Products are consistently delivered, enabling us to be less active. The voices of the medical profession are drowned out by the noises that encourage us to do less and eat more. Research suggests that walking every day for at least 15 minutes is an important factor in improving health. Exercise is one of our best supports in achieving our ideal weight, size and shape.

Addictions

We experience the strength of addiction when we feel forced to eat the chocolate, when we are desperate to open that packet and when we experience a feeling of no choice, of inevitability.

The food industry exists to sell food, and making us go back for more is what the product is designed to do. By recognizing this fact, we are released from feelings of failure and weakness, and with mindfulness we will be able to break this cycle.

Alcohol

Alcohol creates a mind that is open to suggestion and more willing to throw away caution, and is responsible for a lot of bad food choices. Alcohol really has the potential to derail any attempts to change your shape or weight. It is one of the most concentrated sources of calories with little nutritional value. If you want to become more mindful around food, moderating alcohol consumption is a must.

Social pressure

Eating with others is wonderful but we may make choices that we would never make if we were eating alone, and we eat with only a fraction of the awareness that we might usually feel. Knowing this helps you to approach those situations calmly, and by being clear about the choices you have, you can act in accordance with your values and wishes.

Laziness

Even the most efficient and focused person will occasionally think, 'I can't be bothered to cook tonight.' This is where mindfulness comes into play: seeing the feeling and not identifying with it, and so separating it from yourself, will help you to respond with calm. Then you will be more likely to make a healthy choice, instead of simply following the usual habitual patterns.

Sleep

When people are sleeping less, the accumulation of body fat appears to increase – by up to 32 per cent. Also, when people suffer from daytime sleepiness, they are far more likely to crave high-sugar foodstuff. Mindfulness in general might help us to sleep better and to make the positive choices that will help us to avoid weight gain.

Stress

During stress, the mind is on reaction mode as opposed to responding mode. The stress hormone cortisol interferes with the digestion of food, can lead to food cravings and plays a significant part in people putting on weight. It speeds up the accumulation of fat around the waistline, while at the same time breaking down highly prized lean muscle. Mindfulness practices have been shown to trigger the 'relaxation response', a series of physical reactions that are associated with a greater feeling of comfort and ease.

10 steps to mindful eating

1 Listen to your body

Before you pile a mountain of food on your plate or break open a family-sized bag of crisps, take a moment to listen to your physical needs. Are you hungry? If you are, how hungry are you? Serve up just enough food to satisfy the hunger of the body, rather than trying to quench the limitless desire of the mind. You'll be much less likely to go back for more than if you simply had the packet of crisps sitting on your lap.

2 Use smaller serving plates and bowls

Studies have shown that our satisfaction is tied in to 'relative' portion sizes. So, if we have a very small plate that is piled high with food, we will feel much more satisfied than if we have a large plate with a small amount of food – even if the large serving on the small plate contains less! Some new crockery could be the best investment you ever made.

3 Be flexible when eating out

Restaurant menus are generally written in a way that encourages you to eat as much as possible (and why wouldn't they be?) but you don't have to play that game. There is no obligation to have a starter, main course and dessert. Why not have a starter instead of a main course? Why not have tea or coffee instead of a dessert for a change? Oh, and don't be afraid to ask for excess food to be put in a doggie-bag.

4 Serve up at source

When serving food at home, try to plate it up by the oven or hob, rather than at the table. If the excess is on the table in front of you while you are eating, then that's where your mind is likely to be.

Studies have shown that you are likely to eat faster with the excess in front of you. Presumably this is prompted by some survival instinct from the past, when we weren't sure where the next meal was coming from.

5 When you eat, just eat

Portion sizes are intimately related to 'how' we eat. For example, if you sit down at a table with a large box of chocolates and no distractions, you are unlikely to polish off the entire box. This is partly because you would be more aware of hunger levels, but also because you would probably feel greedy, embarrassed or ashamed. But when you're watching TV, surfing the net, or involved in some other activity, this awareness can be drowned out.

6 Learn what a portion size is

If you want to become more mindful of portion sizes, and possibly even to follow the recommended quantities with certain foods, it can be really useful to know and understand what portion sizes are (quite different from 'serving sizes', incidentally, which can be frighteningly large). As a general rule, a 'cup' is about the size of a large tennis ball, 85g of meat comprises the size of a deck of cards and 30g cheese is about the size of a domino. This may help you to avoid having to weigh everything.

7 Think little and often

Many people overeat at meals because they are worried they might feel hungry later on. The body doesn't really work like this and all overeating tends to do is increase the dramatic swings in blood-sugar levels that will,

in all likelihood, have you reaching for the biscuit tin. Try to maintain a stable blood-sugar level and moderate level of satiety by eating small meals throughout the day, rather than just a couple of ridiculously large meals.

8 Have a salad as a starter

We often dive into large portions of rich and colour-dense foods simply because we're hungry. The truth is, in these situations, we're often so hungry that we'd eat just about anything. So be smart and eat some raw vegetables or salad to burn off that extreme hunger before the meal itself. That way you will not feel the same need to overindulge in richer-tasting foods.

9 Have a glass of water before eating

The sensation of thirst is often confused with the feeling of hunger, so that whenever we feel thirsty, we tend to reach out for a snack, or, if about to serve up a meal, we're likely to put more food on the plate. To ensure that you are listening to the right signals, sip a good-sized glass of water in the ten to fifteen minutes leading up to a meal. This way you can be sure that you are serving up only what the body actually needs.

10 Shop smart

Bulk-buying foods can often enable you to pick up some great bargains, but you know your own mind. If you are unable or unwilling to break those down into smaller portion sizes when you get home, then consider the possibility of buying smaller versions. While you may not get the same value for money, take a moment to think of the cost (financial, physical, mental and emotional) of overeating large portions of food.

Frequently used practices

Once we start to engage in a friendly relationship with our bodies, the first foundation of mindfulness, our lives become lighter and more joyful, easy and relaxed. There is no need to fight our body or treat it as an enemy – better to start with a feeling of wonder that you have this body, and that it sustains you day and night. When you are able to accept the body, to respect and love it, you will not only become grateful to be in this body but you will become grateful for all existence.

The body scan

The key objective in doing the body scan is to enhance awareness of physiological sensations and to train your mind to stay focused over a longer than usual period of time on a particular task in the now.

Practise for around forty minutes six times per week, with no expectation or judgment of a particular outcome. Let go of ideas such as success, failure and relaxation, and bring an open mind, curiosity and a sense of adventure to the practice. Lie down on a mat or bed, or sit upright on a chair, and focus for a while on the movement of the breath before directing attention to each region of the body and observing what happens when doing this. Each body scan is a new beginning, a new 'NOW'.

The body scan consists of three steps:
- Intentionally moving the attention to a selected area
- Holding the awareness there and experiencing the sensations
- Moving on.

By regularly practising the body scan you will make some good discoveries:

PAYING ATTENTION is a good practice. Most of us find it relatively easy to focus on our bodies. By paying attention to your body, you make it 'happy' as you trigger its relaxation response.

IT HELPS YOU to reconnect with your body and understand its language.

IT IS A GOOD WAY to be nice to yourself. Remember you are your own best friend. By turning to your body, you are nourishing yourself. You are appreciating it as it is right now, acknowledging that the body serves us day in day out and sustains us in the best possible way. It is our home!

WHEN YOU START to practise body scan, do it in the morning. Normally, when we wake up our minds are not yet busy, so it is easier to focus. Of course, you should choose the time that is best for you – some of us are larks and others are owls.

Here is a brief description of the actual exercise:

TAKE A FEW MOMENTS to get in touch with the movement of your breath and the sensations in your body. Remind yourself of the intention of this practice. Its aim is not to feel any different, relaxed or calm – this may happen or it may not. Instead, the intention of the practice is, as best you can, to bring awareness to any sensations you detect as you focus your attention on each part of the body in turn.

NOW BRING THE FOCUS of your awareness down the left leg, into the left foot. Focus on each of the toes of the left foot in turn, bringing a gentle curiosity to investigating the quality of sensations you find. When you are ready, on an in-breath, feel or imagine the breath entering the lungs, and then passing down into the abdomen, into the left leg, the left foot, and out to the toes of the left foot. Then, on the out-breath, feel or imagine the breath coming all the way back up, out of the foot, into the leg up through the abdomen, chest and out through the nose. Just practise this 'breathing into' as best you can, approaching it playfully.

NEXT ALLOW YOUR AWARENESS to expand into the rest of the foot, then to the ankle, the top of the foot, and right into the bones and joints. Move your awareness to the lower left leg – the calf, shin and knee in turn.

CONTINUE TO BRING AWARENESS, and a gentle curiosity, to the physical sensations in each part of the rest of the body in turn – to the upper left leg, the right toes, right foot, right leg, pelvic area, back, abdomen, chest, fingers, hands, arms, shoulder, neck, head and face. In each area, as best as you can, bring the same detailed level of awareness and gentle curiosity to the bodily sensations present. As you leave each major area, breathe into it on the in-breath, and let go of that region on the out-breath.

WHEN YOU BECOME AWARE of tension, or other intense sensations, in a particular part of the body, you can breathe into that region, using the in-breath gently to bring awareness right into the tension, and, as best as you can, have a sense of letting go, or releasing, on the out-breath.

THE MIND WILL WANDER away from the breath and the body from time to time. That is entirely normal. It is what minds do. When you notice it, acknowledge it, noticing where the mind has gone off to, and then gently return your attention to the body scan.

After you have scanned the whole body in this way, spend a few minutes being aware of the body as a whole, and of the breath flowing freely in and out.

Walking meditation

Walking can be a form of meditation in action, eyes open. The experience of walking is our focus. We are not withdrawing our attention from the outside world to the same extent that we do for the mindfulness of breathing or body-scan practices. Naturally, we have to be aware of obstacles outside of ourselves, and other people. Out of doors, we will be aware of many other things, too – wind, sun, rain and the sounds of nature, humans and machines. One of the biggest differences between sitting inside to meditate and walking outside is that it's easier, for most people, to be more intensely and more easily aware of their bodies while doing walking meditation. When your body is in motion, it is generally easier to be aware of it compared to when you are sitting still. This can make walking meditation a powerful experience, both in becoming aware of your body and in finding profound enjoyment from the practice.

The form of walking meditation described here is best done out of doors. For your first attempt, you might want to find a park or open space where you will be able to walk for 20 minutes without encountering traffic.

• Note your standing posture and the touch sensations of your feet. Let your arms hang naturally.

• As you start walking, keep your attention on the sole of the foot, rather than any other body part. Initially, just notice how you lift, push and drop your foot.

• Thoughts not related to this experience may come up, but just let them go into the background and focus on experiencing walking – notice perhaps how your whole body shifts and adapts with every step.

• If your thoughts become too active, gently let them go, and reconnect with focusing on walking.

Breath-body-thoughts exercise

Our minds sometimes create their own interpretation of events, and this affects our reaction to them. Facts + self-deprecating thoughts = depressive interpretation of events (internal propaganda). Once a negative interpretation stream is started, contrary information is ignored and consistent information is noticed. Therapists used to think that these thoughts were caused by depression. Cognitive therapy teaches the opposite. Negative interpretation causes reduced self-esteem, increased guilt, interrupted concentration and undermined social interaction, plus, possibly, biological effects (stress-response).

• Catch negative thoughts and treat them as hypothesis, not fact. Then seek ways to disprove the hypothesis (reality testing). In this way, we learn to recognize thoughts as thoughts and not as facts.

• Allow thoughts to enter, see how they make you feel/how you interpret them, and then bring your thoughts back to neutrality. Awareness!

• Take a few moments now to become aware of the thoughts that are arising in your mind. Imagine yourself sitting in a cinema, watching an empty screen, just waiting for thoughts to come. When they come, can you see what exactly they are and what happens to them? Some of them will vanish as you become aware of them.

• Focus on specific body reactions and the feelings arising from negative thoughts, such as tension or anger. Observe and stand next to emotion, but do not be dragged down by it.

Everyday informal practices

Every day, remember to do at least one activity mindfully. Here are some examples.

• When you brush your teeth, notice the sensations of the brush on each tooth. Are you thinking about the day or night ahead of you? Notice this and bring your attention back to brushing your teeth.

• In the shower, instead of writing lists in your head or planning a speech for the lunchtime meeting, really feel the water touching your body and be aware of its temperature. Smell the soap or shower gel, notice what it feels like on your skin and feel your muscles relaxing. Then feel gratitude for the luxury of having water just for washing.

• When you hear a sound, any sound – a phone ringing, a passing car, an aeroplane above, a bird singing, a dog barking – kindly remember to embrace this moment and engage for a few minutes in mindful breathing and listening.

The raisin practice

The 'Raisin Experience' was first introduced to the public by Jon Kabat–Zinn, a professor at the University of Massachusetts. This basic practice aims to show us two things:

1. Perception influences taste
2. Heightened awareness can provide us with a richer and more satisfying eating experience.

In the raisin practice you are invited to eat one raisin mindfully, slowly and with awareness of the use of all your senses. Participants often comment on the eye-opening effect this practice can have in relation to their eating patterns. Typical comments are:

'I noticed that no one raisin looks the same in colour, shape and with its ridges.'

'I had a much more pleasurable experience, because the practice of mindfully eating it gave me a heightened sense of its taste, colour and texture.'

'I noticed how much more satisfaction I get out of eating one raisin mindfully compared to my normal habit of eating them one handful at a time.'

'I noticed how often I eat mindlessly, because my mind was all over the place rather than focusing on the food in front of me.'

'I was surprised how it brought back memories from my time as a child with my family, as if it was yesterday.'

'I was surprised how my sense of time changed. Normally I get easily bored, but I was so absorbed in the practice, that I didn't notice the time at all.'

Beforehand

Try to avoid all possible distractions for the time of the practice, such as mobile phones, tablets, reading the newspaper, etc.

Sit and ground yourself by feeling your feet on the floor, your buttocks on the seat. Feel your entire posture. Do you feel tight or loose, collapsed or upright, tired or agitated?

- Connect with your breathing.
- Ask yourself if you are hungry or just fancy a bite to eat.
- Are your thoughts/emotions encouraging you to eat something now?
- Are any of your senses, such as smell or sight, triggering your wish to eat?

Practice

Now look at what's on your plate and imagine that you are seeing it for the first time ever. You could imagine that you are coming from another part of this world, or even from another planet, or you are a small child. This may feel a bit ridiculous, but it is helpful if, for this moment, you try to perceive the items on your plate as if you have never seen them before.

LOOK AT THE COLOURS, the different textures, the forms and the size. Do you see any patterns? If you hold an item of food, either with cutlery or your hands, and turn it around, does it look different from different angles? Is the light reflected differently, showing you light and darker areas? Are there details you didn't notice before?

IF YOU CAN TOUCH IT (raw food, bread, fruits, vegetables, snacks) what do you feel? Is it hard, soft, rough, smooth, wet, dry, sticky, hot, cool, heavy, light? Does it feel the same all over, or are there differences between different parts of it? How do you hold the food? Gently or with tight pressure? Did you notice that your body knows how to pick up food and hold it, without you interfering?

SMELL IT by moving it to your nose. Does it smell sweet, sour, bitter, salty or kind of meaty? Is the smell strong or subtle, or overpowering? Have any memories, associations or images occurred during this part of the practice?

WHEN YOU ARE READY, and when you are willing to do so, put the food into your mouth. You can even place it on your lips to see how that feels. Did you notice the movement of the joints of your hand and arm, and the coordination necessary to bring the food to your mouth? But please, don't chew it yet. Once more feel its texture, weight and taste, and experience how your tongue is moving it. Has the smell intensified? Is the texture changing? What about the taste?

AFTER MOVING it around with your tongue, and when you are ready, start to chew it. Does it make a sound? Does the chewing change the food's texture, taste and moisture? Don't count your bites, let the body chew and let the body decide when to swallow. Does it go down in one big gulp or do you need to swallow several times? Who made the decision to swallow? Your body or you?

THIRTY MINUTES to an hour after the meal, ask yourself: 'How do I feel now?' Are you still hungry or are you satisfied? Are you very full, heavy or light, tired or energized? Knowing this could help you to make better choices next time round.

Getting started –
A sensory recipe experience

Guided practice –Thai veg salad

All five senses are involved in wanting food, and enjoying it – taste, smell, sight, sound and touch. They work together to give us a complete sensory experience, enabling us to savour our food.

Simply thinking of food can make you hungry. The following recipe will introduce you to the process of mindful eating, focusing on each sense to guide you through the basic principles.

1 This recipe is simple and will take just ten minutes to cook plus cooling time. It is full of bright and colourful ingredients to awaken the sense of sight, a wide variety of textures to explore, aromatic herbs and, most importantly, it has a fantastic, fresh taste. Take time to display and garnish the food so it looks appetizing – a dish you are proud of having prepared. Enjoy the exotic brightness and interesting layers.

2 When making the dressing, take the time to sample the flavours – the sourness of the lime and the saltiness of the soy sauce, for example. Remember to use as many of your senses as possible. As the ingredients warm, smell the sweet comforting marmalade and spicy chilli.

3 Really look at the salad ingredients while you are preparing them. Notice texture and colour. What does the food feel like? Is it hard or soft? Grainy or sticky? Moist or dry? Enjoy the sound and sensation of chopping different shapes and surfaces. Crush a herb leaf in your fingers. Does that release the aroma? How do the spring onions contrast with the sweet, peppery mango?

4 As you toss the salad in the dressing, notice how the ingredients combine to make a different set of textures and smells.

5 Take small mouthfuls and at least two minutes to finish each one. Chew as slowly as possible to give yourself time to experience each sensation. Close your eyes and concentrate on the smell, the taste and the texture.

6 Notice the peanuts, the way they crunch and crumble in your mouth. How does the saltiness of the soy sauce bring out the sweet flavour burst of a cherry tomato? What is your favourite ingredient? Do you like the chilli kick or the freshness of the Lebanese cucumber? Notice if the intensity of the flavours change, and concentrate on the sensation of swallowing.

Thai veg salad

Calories per serving 180
Serves 4
Preparation time 10 minutes,
  plus cooling
Cooking time 2 minutes

250 g (8 oz) cherry tomatoes,
  quartered
1 Lebanese cucumber, thinly sliced
1 green papaya or green mango
1 large red chilli, deseeded and
  thinly sliced
150 g (5 oz) bean sprouts
4 spring onions, thinly sliced
small handful of Thai basil leaves
small handful of mint leaves
small handful of fresh
  coriander leaves
4 tablespoons unsalted peanuts,
  roughly chopped

Chilli dressing
2 tablespoons sweet chilli sauce
2 tablespoons light soy sauce
2 tablespoons lime juice
2 tablespoons lime marmalade,
  warmed

Make the dressing. Put all the ingredients in a small saucepan
and warm over a low heat, stirring, until combined. Leave
to cool.

Put the tomatoes, cucumber, papaya or mango, chilli, bean
sprouts, spring onions and herbs in a bowl. Add the dressing
and toss well. Transfer to a platter. Sprinkle over the peanuts
and serve immediately.

Smell

Our sense of smell is more closely related to how things taste than any other sense; 75 per cent of what we perceive as taste comes from our sense of smell. When we say a meal tasted good, we might not know that a great part of this is due to our experience of its smell.

When we put food in our mouths, odour molecules from the food travel to olfactory receptor cells at the top of the nasal cavity, which sits just beneath the brain. The olfactory bulb is part of the brain's limbic system, also called the emotional brain. The olfactory bulb has access to the amygdala, which processes emotion, and the hippocampus, which is responsible for associative learning. When we have a cold, we can't taste much. This is due to the build-up of mucus in the nasal passage preventing the odour molecules from reaching the olfactory receptor cells. The brain receives no signal and we experience the food as tasteless. Thus when the sense of smell doesn't work, the sense of taste is not triggered. When children are made to eat food or take medicine they don't like, or that tastes bitter, they hold their nose and gulp it down fast to avoid tasting it.

Smell can bring back a flood of memories and has a very powerful effect on mood and emotion. Our emotional repertoire can remind us of characteristic smells associated with places and activities in the past. For example, the smell of strong disinfectant can remind you of hospital visits you made as a child. If you encounter that smell later in life, it can trigger feelings of loneliness and abandonment.

Explore smell *Lemon & cardamom madeleines*

Calories per serving 80

Makes about 30

Preparation time 20 minutes,
plus setting

Cooking time 30 minutes

125 g (4 oz) lightly salted butter,
melted, plus extra for greasing
125 g (4 oz) self-raising flour,
plus extra for dusting
2 teaspoons cardamom pods
3 eggs
125 g (4 oz) caster sugar
finely grated zest of 1 lemon
½ teaspoon baking powder

Glaze

2 tablespoons lemon juice
75 g (3 oz) icing sugar, sifted,
plus extra for dusting

AWARENESS POINTS

- Cardamom seeds are intensely aromatic when crushed. Green pods are sweet flavoured and are used in making Garam Masala Chai. Black pods have a smokier aroma.
- Notice the fresh, zingy smell of the lemon before and after you grate the rind.
- The smell of baking is one of the most comforting and appetizing. Use the half-hour aking time to savour positive feelings.

Grease a madeleine tray with melted butter and dust with flour. Tap out the excess flour.

Crush the cardamom pods using a pestle and mortar to release the seeds. Remove the shells and crush the seeds a little further.

Put the eggs, caster sugar, lemon zest and crushed cardamom seeds in a heatproof bowl and rest the bowl over a saucepan of gently simmering water. Whisk with a hand-held electric whisk until the mixture is thick and pale and the mixture leaves a trail when lifted.

Sift the flour and baking powder into the bowl and gently fold in using a large metal spoon. Drizzle the melted butter around the edges of the mixture and fold the ingredients together to combine. Spoon the mixture into the madeleine sections until about two-thirds full. (Keep the remaining mixture for a second batch.)

Bake in a preheated oven, 220°C (425°F), Gas Mark 7, for about 10 minutes until risen and golden. Leave in the tray for 5 minutes, then transfer to a wire rack.

Make the glaze by putting the lemon juice in a bowl and beating in the icing sugar. Brush over the madeleines and leave to set. Serve lightly dusted with icing sugar.

Sight

Sight is a trigger for appetite and does not affect the ability to taste, although it influences our perception of taste. For example, some studies show that a darker colour makes us think a drink is stronger. When food looks fresh and is well presented, it triggers our taste buds and saliva glands. A well-presented buffet leads us to anticipate a tasty meal. If the buffet looks drab, the salad is limp and the food is colourless, we are less inclined to have positive expectations.

The main reason for sight's influence is memory of past experiences with colour and flavour. We remember what fresh bread looks like compared with mouldy bread. We can identify vegetables and fruits that are fresh, those that are past their best and those that are unripe. We go for the yellow banana, not the green. We choose the brown/green apple for sour taste, the red apple for sweet taste.

TIP

If the chocolate bar or crisp packet is left on the coffee table in front of the TV, chances are you won't resist. Put it away and replace it with some healthier options, such as carrot sticks, or apples and grapes with cheese. Remember, out of sight is out of mind. Put healthy food in a prime position; ideally, unhealthy food should be hidden.

Memory influences our food choices. If we have had a good experience with certain food, we think it looks good. If we have no experience with it, our minds will try to associate it with something familiar. We might avoid a specific food because we don't recognize it and it looks strange, weird even, and not very appetizing. We might think we know how it tastes just by looking at it. But we might be mistaken.

If you are hungry, the mind recognizes the overriding need for food and makes you select something, even if it doesn't look that enticing. So try something that looks unfamiliar to you. You might feel better because you stepped out of autopilot, happier and empowered. Feeling happier means you can make better choices.

Explore sight *Tomato & mozzarella salad*

Calories per serving 212
Serves 4
Preparation time 15 minutes

500 g (1 lb) ripe tomatoes, preferably
    different types, such as heirloom
    and cherry and plum
about 3 tablespoons olive oil
2 tablespoons aged balsamic vinegar
small handful of basil leaves
150 g (5 oz) mini mozzarella balls
salt and pepper

Cut half the tomatoes into thick
slices and the other half into wedges.
Arrange the slices on a large serving
plate, slightly overlapping each other.

Put the tomato wedges in a bowl and
drizzle with most of the olive oil and
balsamic vinegar. Season to taste with
salt and pepper. Mix carefully and
arrange on top of the tomato slices.

Add the basil leaves and mozzarella
balls to the tomato wedges. Drizzle the
salad with more olive oil and balsamic
vinegar, season to taste with salt and
pepper and serve.

AWARENESS POINTS

- Make it your mission to choose as many different
  tomatoes as possible – home-grown or shop bought,
  you can create a full spectrum of red colours.
- Notice the way the balsamic sinks in to the intricate
  tears in the mozzarella. Imagine how it will add to
  the flavour.
- Think about presentation. Notice how the layering
  of ingredients adds to the impression of the dish.

Sound

Food comes with its own sounds. Think of those we make when we are eating – we chomp, crunch, grind, gulp, gnaw, munch, slurp, sputter, choke maybe, burp even. The crunchiness of crisps, for example, has become an essential part of our enjoyment of them, and our perception of them as fresh. We think the louder they crunch, the fresher the crisps.

The sound of calming music can make you feel peaceful and relaxed, and encourage you to stay longer at a restaurant and order another drink, or possibly a dessert. Even if you know that, I guess you may not know that sound can modulate taste, so that food tastes sweeter or more bitter, depending on the music you are listening to. Welcome to the science of 'sonic seasoning'.

We might think that sound has little or no impact on our eating habits, but think twice. What about the sound of the sizzling sausage in the pan, the sound of hot water boiling for the first cup of tea, the gurgling sound of the coffee machine, the crunchy crisps, the sound of nuts cracking, the squelchy sound of a ripe peach?

Our brain recognizes the food by remembering the sounds of food we have eaten in the past. It recognizes loudness, pitch and type, and once it has confirmed the memory of the sound, it will begin to fire up the part of the brain that desires the item.

Explore sound *Peach & blueberry crunch*

Calories per serving 371
Serves 4
Preparation time 8 minutes
Cooking time 8–10 minutes

25 g (1 oz) ground hazelnuts
25 g (1 oz) ground almonds
25 g (1 oz) caster sugar
25 g (1 oz) breadcrumbs
410 g (13½ oz) can peaches
   in natural juice
125 g (4 oz) blueberries
150 ml (¼ pint) double cream
seeds from 1 vanilla pod
1 tablespoon icing sugar, sifted

Gently cook the ground nuts in a large frying pan with the sugar and breadcrumbs, stirring constantly until golden. Remove from the heat and leave to cool.

Put the peaches in a food processor or blender and blend with enough of the peach juice to make a thick, smooth purée.

Set aside some of the blueberries to decorate and fold the remaining blueberries gently into the purée. Spoon into 4 glasses or individual serving dishes.

Whip the cream with the vanilla seeds and icing sugar until thick but not stiff and spoon evenly over the peach purée. When the crunchy topping is cool, sprinkle it over the blueberry mixture, top with the remaining blueberries and serve.

AWARENESS POINTS

- Apply the raisin experience (see page 18) to an almond. When you slowly eat the almond, where can you hear the crunch, in what parts of your head and ears?
- What noise do the ground nuts make in the frying pan. Do they hiss or rustle when the pan is shaken?
- How does the creaminess of the blueberry mixture effect the sound of the nuts when you eat them?

Touch

Touch is integral to our experience with food. It informs us about texture, moisture, chewiness, greasiness, whether the food is likely to be painful (hot chilli) or astringent. By touching we know if a peach is ripe or not, we sense the smoothness of the apple, the roughness of the pear, the waxed surface of the lemon/orange, we feel if the food is heavy or light, hot or cold, wet or dry. All this information is carried to the brain where it is assessed, stimulating desire or dislike, so that we know to wait for the drink to cool down, or the peach to ripen before eating it.

Touch influences our perception of taste, too. Bread that is hard, even if the taste and smell are okay, is not pleasant. We won't eat cold porridge; some people don't like lukewarm milk or the feeling of edible cactus.

Explore touch *Layered nutty bars*

Calories per serving 406
Cuts into 10
Preparation time 20 minutes,
  plus chilling
Cooking time 5 minutes

50 g (2 oz) butter
400 g (13 oz) fat-free sweetened
  condensed milk
200 g (7 oz) plain dark chocolate,
  broken into pieces
125 g (4 oz) rich tea biscuits
50 g (2 oz) hazelnuts
100 g (3½ oz) pistachio nuts, shelled

Use a little of the butter to grease the base and sides of a
20 cm (8 inch) round spring-form tin. Put the rest of the butter
in a saucepan with the condensed milk and chocolate. Heat
gently for 3–4 minutes, stirring until melted, then remove
from the heat.

Place the biscuits in a plastic bag and crush roughly into
chunky pieces using a rolling pin. Toast the hazelnuts under
a preheated hot grill until lightly browned, then roughly chop
with the pistachios.

Stir the biscuits into the chocolate mixture, then spoon half
the mixture into the prepared tin and spread level. Reserve
2 tablespoons of the nuts for the top, then sprinkle the rest
over the chocolate biscuit layer. Cover with the remaining
chocolate mixture, level the surface with the back of the spoon
and sprinkle with the reserved nuts.

Chill the nut mixture for 3–4 hours until firm, then loosen the
edges and remove the sides of the tin. Cut into 10 thin slices,
or into tiny bite-sized pieces to make petits fours. Store any
leftovers in the refrigerator, wrapped in foil, for up to 3 days.

AWARENESS POINTS
- This baking recipe is great for getting your hands messy
  and really connecting with the food.
- Use your hands to grease the tin, noticing the coolness
  of the metal.
- As you add each layer of nuts and biscuits to the tray,
  carefully push into place with your fingers, exploring
  and comparing the rough textures.

Taste

Flavour is important to us and what we call taste is the interconnected experience of several senses, especially smell and touch, into one single experience. When we put food into our mouth, the taste receptors on the tongue and the roof of the mouth (the taste buds) send an impulse to the brain through the cranial nerve. The brain then compares the information with stored memory of previous tastes and recognizes what you are eating. After that, it will decide if you like the taste of the food or drink, and if it is a good idea to continue consuming it.

We used to refer to four tastes – sweet, bitter, sour and salty – but recently another one, umami, has been recognized. This is found in fermented and aged foods, such as cheese and tamari (a gluten-free variety of soy sauce from Japan), and is savoury.

It was once thought that these tastes were centred on different areas of the tongue but this is now no longer considered to be true. Each taste bud, no matter where it sits on the tongue, has the potential to pick up any of the five known tastes.

Explore taste *Fennel & orange casserole*

Calories per serving 232
  (not including polenta)
Serves 4
Preparation time 15 minutes
Cooking time about 50 minutes

2 fennel bulbs, trimmed
4 tablespoons extra-virgin olive oil
1 onion, chopped
2 garlic cloves, crushed
2 teaspoons chopped rosemary
100 ml (3½ fl oz) Pernod
400 g (13 oz) can chopped tomatoes
¼ teaspoon saffron threads
2 strips of orange rind
2 tablespoons chopped fennel fronds
salt and pepper

Cut the fennel lengthways into 5 mm (¼ inch) thick slices. Heat half the oil in a flameproof casserole, add the fennel slices, in batches, and cook over a medium heat for 3–4 minutes on each side until golden. Remove with a slotted spoon.

Heat the remaining oil in the casserole, add the onion, garlic, rosemary and salt and pepper and cook over a low heat, stirring frequently, for 5 minutes. Add the Pernod, bring to the boil and boil until reduced by half. Add the tomatoes, saffron and orange rind and stir well. Arrange the fennel slices over the top.

Bring to the boil, then cover the casserole with a tightfitting lid and bake in a preheated oven, 180°C (350°F), Gas Mark 4, for 35 minutes until the fennel is tender. Stir in the fennel fronds and serve the casserole hot with chargrilled polenta triangles, if liked.

AWARENESS POINTS

- Compare the taste of the fennel before and after cooking in stage one.
- Taste the sauce five times, focusing on, in turn, the garlic, rosemary, salt, pernod and orange.
- Does saffron have a taste? How would you describe it?

Breath: past, future & eating in the 'now'

To learn to be with the present is not for the faint-hearted. It takes courage, because it can be painful and frightening when, for example, we have just stuffed down another bout of food. To learn to be present with kind attention, we use the breath. It is always with us, easy to track and accessible, and absolutely free. As the breath occurs only in the now, using it is an excellent way to stay present and to remind us to connect with our reality.

It is true for most of us that, for a big part of our lives, we have lived more in the past or in the future than in the present moment. Unfortunately, thinking of the past or the future will make us more stressed and agitated since we can't do anything about either of them in this moment. Hence we tend to look for something to soothe us, often food or drink.

It can be helpful to reflect on past events, so we can gain insight into what we did and why we did it, in case we need to do things differently now. Thinking about doing it differently is happening in the present moment. However, by the time we are doing it differently, it is already taking place in a new present moment (which was the future when we first thought about it). We often tend to be trapped in repetitive, negative or attached thinking about the past and future. This can trigger a low mood, remembering all the highlights and good times we had (attachment), which alas have gone now and may never return; or it can fill us with regret (another type of low mood) about what we have done wrong or missed doing.

The future is also important, because our aspirations and intentions give us direction. Only when we know what we aspire to can we collect our energies and move towards our goal. But even if we know our goal, the first step and all those that follow happen in the present moment.

We can dream, hope and have wonderful fantasies, but we still have to take one step at a time, and each step is occurring in the present moment. Thinking about the future can also trigger low mood, as we might compare the much more colourful and successful future of what 'might be' with the reality of what actually is. Reality often lacks the splendour of our imagination.

Wherever you are at this moment, that's where you are. That is your starting point. The past is gone and the future is not yet here. It is only in this moment that we can make new and healthier choices. It is in this moment that we can start again and decide the direction of our eating life.

Experimenting with the breath

(This is largely based on breath awareness as taught by Thanissaro Bhikku.)

Sit down comfortably and keep warm. Where do you feel the breath right now?

Is it shallow or deep, long or short, fast or slow? Has it got a rhythm? What kind of rhythm would make you feel really good?

How can you receive the breath in your body, in the lungs and the belly, that is pleasant, enjoyable and soothing?

See what works for you.

Try to think of the breath flowing through the entire body like waves of energy – in through the toes and up to the head, touching along its way all the nerves, blood vessels, bones.

While you are feeling the breath flowing like this, are there areas in the body where it feels blocked? What helps to unblock these areas? Breathing through them, around them or straight into them? See what works for you. Play with the breath and discover the impact of the breath on your mind.

Notice that you are aware of your breath and you are aware of the effect it has on your wellbeing.

When you have found the breath pattern that gives you a sense of fullness and ease, be aware that your mind is now centred and calm.

Notice that you are aware of your breath and calm mind and now turn to awareness itself.

The more often you try this, the more often you will be able to access a calm and centred mind in your life, and also during shopping and eating.

TIPS

Bigger portions make us eat more – up to 30 per cent. So be clever. Use smaller plates and smaller glasses and increase the volume of your food through extra air and water. Air and water are the cheapest ingredients to bulk up your food without adding a calorie to it. In a research project, one group of people ate fresh fruit and another group drank smoothies made with the same amount of fruit. Those who drank the smoothie felt fuller because it had been stirred for a short while and contained more volume through the air that had been whisked into it.

Don't finish all the food on your plate. For generations brought up during and after the war, this is anathema. Their parents, quite rightly, cherished food. But in some cultures, hosts stop offering you more food only when you leave some on the plate, signalling that you are full. Practise not clearing your plate and it will help you to develop the self-control you need to stop overeating, and help you to eat less.

Guided practice

Smoothies are a great way to consume food mindfully. They rely on nutritious ingredients, such as fruit and milk or live yogurt, which nourish our bodies and provide healthy energy. They can include honey for sweetness, or avocado for savoury creaminess, and it's easy to vary the recipe to omit dairy products if you prefer. Whisked to provide an airy lightness, smoothies can be sipped and savoured, and are filling without being heavy.

1 We breathe deeply when we smell something pleasant. As you begin to make this smoothie, savour the delicious aroma of the sweet berries as you prepare them. Enjoy the heady scent of ripe peaches as you cut into them and release their juice. How does the skin feel to touch? When you chop fruit, or use a noisy blender to mix the ingredients or crush ice, do you hold your breath?

2 Notice your breathing, and try to keep it slow and mindful. Appreciate the anticipation of the exotic flavour combinations, and choose a suitable glass to display the bright colour of this energy-providing power drink.

3 How will you drink it? Will you sip it through a straw? Perhaps you could sit outside and enjoy the fresh air, if the weather is good enough.

4 It can be hard to drink mindfully, especially when you are thirsty. Being dehydrated can lead to consuming your meals much too fast, which in turn leads to overindulgence. Drink a large glass of water before you begin, to rehydrate your body and allow yourself to tune in to what your body requires.

5 Remember to savour the smell of the fruit as you begin to drink the smoothie. Notice the creaminess, the sharp tang of the fruit, the sweetness and the pleasant chill from the ice. Were you too hot when you started drinking it? Can you feel the cool sensation travelling through your chest, refreshing your body? Pause, and breathe deeply and mindfully between each mouthful.

6 Although blended, a smoothie is still nourishing, satisfying food, and it is important to notice when your stomach is full. When you have finished, return to the breath, and to stillness.

Fruity summer smoothie

Calories per serving 103
Makes 4 x 300 ml (½ pint) glasses
Preparation time 2 minutes

2 peaches, halved, stoned and chopped
300 g (10 oz) strawberries, hulled
300 g (10 oz) raspberries
400 ml (14 fl oz) skimmed
    or semi-skimmed milk
ice cubes

Put the peaches in a blender or food processor with the strawberries and raspberries and blend to a smooth purée, scraping the mixture down from the sides of the bowl if necessary.

Add the milk and blend the ingredients again until the mixture is smooth and frothy. Pour the milkshake over the ice cubes in 4 tall glasses.

Breakfast

The intelligent body

'Those who know when they have enough will not be disgraced;
Those who know how to stop will not be harmed.'

LAO TZU

Lost in autopilot

It seems that we have lost the ability to feel the signals the body is sending us to indicate that it is full. The body does not require calorie tables, because it knows perfectly well when to stop.

Paying attention to bodily sensations is a central part of mindful eating. As we increase our awareness, we learn to read the signs and to stop when we are full. Being in your body means you are in the present moment. It is in the now that you can feel your hunger. Unfortunately, people often eat for the future. Some people say they were eating even when they were not hungry, just to make sure they would not be hungry later in the day. By getting in touch with the body, you will relearn how it feels when you are hungry and when you are full.

The loss of innocence

Our relationship with our bodies has become complicated. We are judgmental, especially regarding image and shape – the body is ugly, disgusting, loathsome, yuk, frumpy, a blob, sordid, weak. We listen to other people talking and as we feel rejected, so we reject ourselves. By talking to ourselves like this, we miss hearing or sensing the body's subtle voice. Relearning to take notice of a light pressure in the stomach or some slight difficulty breathing as we get fuller is one of the most important goals in rebalancing our weight. Occasionally, the body's voice gets louder, or even screams. We may be feeling sick, overfull, uncomfortable. We have problems with digestion, develop heartburn. Unfortunately, most of us, most of the time, are not truly present in our bodies.

It wasn't always like this. In our childhood we didn't worry about our basic needs or how to fulfil them. The body and its innate intelligence took care of it. We slept when we were tired, and we cried when we needed food or cuddles. Our body was tirelessly and reliably working for us and supporting us as it was turning food into blood, bones and tissue. That is what we call the intelligence of the original body.

You may wonder what causes the loss of this simple and straightforward relationship with our body that was once a natural part of life. The answer is simple and yet hard to believe. The loss occurs through the process of growing up and being taught about 'civilized' behaviour, including how we should walk, sit, conduct ourselves and dress according to our gender, age, class and culture. Mindfulness aims to bring the body and its sensations back into the field of our awareness so that once again we can feel its natural ability to pulse and flow with life.

Guided practice

1 Start the day as you mean to go on and be as kind to your body as possible. Oats are a good source of slow-release carbohydrates, and porridge is something we associate with comfort, warmth and sharing. You can vary the first recipe here by adding seeds, different fruits, honeys and syrups – it is a great dish to leave you feeling full and satisfied.

2 Everyone has their own personal preference when it comes to porridge consistency so enjoy the sensation of stirring the milk and watching the oats thicken. Choose your favourite bowl and spoon – perhaps someone gave them to you as a gift, they have strong memories attached or you like the shape and colour.

3 When you sit down to eat, take a moment to assess how your body feels. Register any feelings of tension. Pay attention in turn to your mouth, throat, chest and stomach. Are you too hot or cold? Do you need to open the window or put on a jumper before you start eating? Is your stomach rumbling? Is the smell of delicious porridge making your mouth water? Have you had a glass of water – perhaps you are dehydrated?

4 Sit up straight, pick up the spoon carefully and bring one small spoonful to your mouth. Test how hot it is. As you eat the first mouthful, concentrate on the sensation of the porridge in your mouth. Is it creamy? Is it coarse? Is the consistency just how you like it? Notice how it warms your throat, down through your chest and into your stomach.

5 Recent studies say it takes twenty minutes before we register the feeling of fullness, so take as long to finish as possible. Savour every spoonful. See how the feeling of hunger changes and lessens. Perhaps you don't need to eat the whole bowl of porridge? It is all right not to finish your meal; next time you'll know to make a smaller portion. You could try pausing and putting down your spoon between mouthfuls.

6 Finally, compare how you feel now with when you started your breakfast. Do you feel full and satisfied? Is your body less tense? Enjoy the feeling of being full, but not too full – just right.

Porridge & prune compote

Calories per serving 259
Serves 8
Preparation time 5 minutes
Cooking time about 20 minutes

1 litre (1¾ pints) skimmed
or semi-skimmed milk
1 teaspoon vanilla extract
pinch of ground cinnamon
pinch of salt
200 g (7 oz) porridge oats
3 tablespoons flaked almonds, toasted

Compote
250 g (8 oz) ready-to-eat dried Agen prunes
125 ml (4 fl oz) apple juice
1 small cinnamon stick
1 clove
1 tablespoon runny honey
1 unpeeled orange quarter

Place all the compote ingredients in a small saucepan over a medium heat. Simmer gently for 10–12 minutes or until softened and slightly sticky. Leave to cool. (The compote can be prepared in advance and chilled.)

Put the milk, 500 ml (17 fl oz) water, vanilla extract, cinnamon and salt in a large saucepan over a medium heat and bring slowly to the boil. Stir in the oats, then reduce the heat and simmer gently, stirring occasionally, for 8–10 minutes until creamy and tender. Spoon the porridge into warmed bowls, scatter with the almonds and serve with the prune compote.

Asparagus with smoked salmon

Calories per serving 150
Serves 6
Preparation time 10 minutes
Cooking time 6 minutes

200 g (7 oz) trimmed asparagus
3 tablespoons roughly chopped
   hazelnuts
4 teaspoons olive oil
juice of 1 lime
1 teaspoon Dijon mustard
12 quail eggs
250 g (8 oz) smoked salmon
salt and pepper

AWARENESS POINTS

- Notice the fresh green of the asparagus and how it brightens as it steams
- Take your time arranging the food on the plate, and be creative – enjoy yourself!
- Mark the rich flavour of the quail eggs, the salty bite of the salmon and the tang of the lime.

Steam the asparagus spears over a saucepan of boiling water for 5 minutes until just tender.

Meanwhile, grill the nuts on a piece of foil until lightly browned. Lightly mix together the oil, lime juice and mustard with a little salt and pepper, then stir in the hot nuts. Keep warm.

Pour water into a saucepan to a depth of 4 cm (1½ inches) and bring it to the boil. Lower the eggs into the water with a slotted spoon and cook for 1 minute. Take the pan off the heat and leave the eggs to stand for 1 minute. Drain the eggs, rinse with cold water and drain again.

Tear the salmon into strips and divide it among 6 serving plates, folding and twisting the strips attractively. Tuck the just-cooked asparagus into the salmon, halve the quail eggs, leaving the shells on if liked, and arrange on top. Drizzle with the warm nut dressing and serve sprinkled with a little black pepper.

Cranberry muffins

Calories per muffin 172
Makes 12
Preparation time 10 minutes
Cooking time 18–20 minutes

150 g (5 oz) plain flour
150 g (5 oz) self-raising flour
1 tablespoon baking powder
65 g (2½ oz) light muscovado sugar
3 pieces stem ginger from a jar,
   about 50 g (2 oz), finely chopped
100 g (3½oz) dried cranberries
1 egg
250 ml (8 fl oz) milk
4 tablespoons vegetable oil

AWARENESS POINTS

- Use decorative muffin cases in your favourite colour or pattern.
- Try the raisin experience (see page 18) with a dried cranberry. Experience the sweetness and the texture slowly and mindfully.
- How does the warm smell of baking muffins change your mood?

Line a 12-hole muffin tin with paper muffin cases. Sift the flours and baking powder into a large bowl. Stir in the sugar, ginger and cranberries until evenly distributed.

Beat together the egg, milk and oil in a separate bowl, then add the liquid to the flour mixture. Using a large metal spoon, gently stir the liquid into the flour until only just combined. The mixture should look craggy, with specks of flour still visible.

Divide the mixture evenly among the muffin cases, piling it up in the centre. Bake in a preheated oven, 200°C (400°F), Gas Mark 6, for 18–20 minutes until well risen and golden. Transfer to a wire rack and serve while still slightly warm.

For wholemeal apricot & orange muffins, replace the plain flour with 150 g (5 oz) wholemeal flour. Use 100 g (3½ oz) chopped ready-to-eat dried apricots instead of the cranberries and omit the ginger. Fold the finely grated rind of 1 orange into the mixture before baking.

Spinach & butter bean frittata

Calories per serving 432
  (not including salad)

Serves 2

Preparation time 10 minutes

Cooking time 10 minutes

1 teaspoon olive oil

1 onion, sliced

400 g (13 oz) can butter beans, rinsed
  and drained

200 g (7 oz) baby spinach leaves

4 eggs, beaten

50 g (2 oz) ricotta cheese

salt (optional) and black pepper

Heat the oil in a medium frying pan. Add the onion and fry for 3–4 minutes until softened. Add the butter beans and spinach and heat gently for 2–3 minutes until the spinach has wilted.

Pour over the eggs, then spoon over the ricotta and season with salt (if liked) and pepper. Cook until almost set, then place under a preheated hot grill and cook for 1–2 minutes until golden and set. Serve with a tomato and red onion salad, if liked.

AWARENESS POINTS

- Observe how the surface of the frittata changes colour and texture under the grill.
- This is a very quick breakfast to prepare, so use the extra time to eat the meal slowly and mindfully.
- Beans and eggs are a great source of fibre and protein. Notice the point where you are full.

Corn & bacon muffins

Calories per muffin 228

Makes 12

Preparation time 10 minutes

Cooking time 15–20 minutes

3 tablespoons vegetable oil,
  plus extra for greasing

6 streaky bacon rashers

1 small red onion, finely chopped

200 g (7 oz) frozen sweetcorn

175 g (6 oz) fine cornmeal

125 g (4 oz) plain flour

2 teaspoons baking powder

50 g (2 oz) Cheddar cheese, grated

200 ml (7 fl oz) milk

2 eggs

AWARENESS POINTS

- Take a moment to really appreciate the sizzling sounds of frying bacon and onions.
- Perhaps you could serve the muffins with a sprig of coriander or some sliced cherry tomatoes for contrast.
- How does the texture and the flavour of a warm muffin compare to a cool one?

Lightly oil a 12-hole muffin tin. Cut off any rind and excess fat, then finely chop the bacon and dry-fry it in a pan with the onion over a medium heat for 3–4 minutes until the bacon turns crisp. Cook the sweetcorn in boiling water for 2 minutes to soften.

Put the cornmeal, flour and baking powder in a bowl and mix together. Add the sweetcorn, cheese, bacon and onions, and stir in.

Whisk the milk with the eggs and oil and add to the bowl. Stir gently until combined, then divide among the tin sections.

Bake in a preheated oven, 220°C (425°F), Gas Mark 7, for 15–20 minutes until golden and just firm. Loosen the edges of the muffins with a knife and transfer to a wire rack to cool.

Banana & sultana drop scones

Calories per serving 110
Makes 10
Preparation time 10 minutes
Cooking time 8 minutes

125 g (4 oz) self-raising flour
2 tablespoons caster sugar
½ teaspoon baking powder
1 small ripe banana, about
   125 g (4 oz) with skin on,
   peeled and roughly mashed
1 egg, beaten
150 ml (¼ pint) milk
50 g (2 oz) sultanas
oil, for greasing
butter, clear honey, or golden
   or maple syrup, to serve

Put the flour, sugar and baking powder in a mixing bowl. Add the mashed banana with the egg. Gradually whisk in the milk with a fork until the mixture resembles a smooth, thick batter. Stir in the sultanas.

Pour a little oil on to a piece of folded kitchen paper and use to grease a griddle or heavy nonstick frying pan. Heat the pan, then drop heaped dessertspoonfuls of the mixture, well spaced apart, on to the pan. Cook for 2 minutes until bubbles appear on the top and the undersides are golden. Turn over and cook for a further 1–2 minutes until cooked.

Serve warm, each topped with 1 teaspoon butter, honey, golden or maple syrup. These are best eaten on the day they are made.

AWARENESS POINTS

- Notice the sweet smell of the ripe banana before you make the scones.
- Mark the changing texture as you whisk the mixture – is there a point at which it begins to require more effort?
- Taste the topping options, one at a time, with your eyes closed, and decide which you prefer.

Guided practice

A cooked breakfast tends to signify an occasion. Eggs play a huge part in any celebratory breakfast or brunch and are a great protein-rich way to start the day. Take the time to appreciate where the eggs have come from. Have you checked they are reliably sourced? More and more people are keeping chickens and growing their own food stuff so perhaps these eggs come from even closer to home.

1 Notice the way the smells in the kitchen change as you add the ingredients to the hot pan. How does it affect your appetite? How long before the onion and garlic start to sizzle? Ras El Hanout is extremely distinctive - does it evoke any memories of travels or other Moroccan dishes you may have tried? What do you notice about the texture of the coriander and how does it change when it begins to cook?

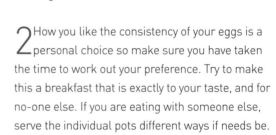

2 How you like the consistency of your eggs is a personal choice so make sure you have taken the time to work out your preference. Try to make this a breakfast that is exactly to your taste, and for no-one else. If you are eating with someone else, serve the individual pots different ways if needs be.

3 Make every bite count. See if you can distinguish the sharpness of the cherry tomatoes against the garlic and ras el hanout. How would you describe the taste of the yolk compared to the cooked egg white? With the next bite see if you can you make out the very subtle pinch of cinnamon.

Moroccan baked eggs

Calories per serving 170
Serves 2
Preparation time 10 minutes
Cooking time 25–35 minutes

½ tablespoon olive oil
½ onion, chopped
1 garlic clove, sliced
½ teaspoon ras el hanout
pinch ground cinnamon
½ teaspoon ground coriander
400 g (13 oz) cherry tomatoes
2 tablespoons chopped coriander leaves
2 eggs
salt and pepper

Heat the oil in a frying pan over a medium heat, add the onion and garlic and cook for 6–7 minutes or until softened and lightly golden, stirring occasionally. Stir in the spices and cook for a further 1 minute. Add the tomatoes and season well with salt and pepper, then simmer gently for 8–10 minutes. Scatter over 3 teaspoons of the coriander, then divide the tomato mixture among 2 individual ovenproof dishes. Break an egg into each dish.

Bake in a preheated oven, 220°C (425°F), Gas Mark 7, for 8–10 minutes until the egg is set but the yolks are still slightly runny. Cook for a further 2–3 minutes if you prefer the eggs to be cooked through. Serve scattered with the remaining coriander.

Figs with yogurt & honey

Calories per serving 105
Serves 4
Preparation time 5 minutes
Cooking time 10 minutes

8 ripe figs
4 tablespoons natural yogurt
2 tablespoons clear honey

Slice the figs in half and place on a hot griddle pan, skin-side down. Sear for 10 minutes until the skins begin to blacken, then remove.

Arrange the figs on 4 plates and serve with a spoonful of yogurt and the honey spooned over the top.

For brioche French toasts with figs, yogurt & honey, brush 4 slices of brioche with a mixture of 50 g (2 oz) melted butter and 50 ml (2 fl oz) single cream and toast under a preheated grill. Top with figs, as above.

AWARENESS POINTS

- Notice the beautiful natural shape of the split figs.
- Take a slow mouthful of fig, honey and yogurt. Enjoy the contrast of the fibrous fruit with the sticky sweet honey and the sharp, sour yogurt.
- Think about the energy and the nutrition you will gain from eating this healthy, luxurious breakfast.

Nutty passion fruit yogurts

Calories per serving 348

Serves 2

Preparation time 5 minutes,
   plus chilling

2 passion fruit

250 ml (8 fl oz) natural yogurt

4 tablespoons clear honey

50 g (2 oz) hazelnuts, toasted and
   roughly chopped

4 clementines, peeled and chopped
   into small pieces

AWARENESS POINTS

- Touch the various textures
  of the passion fruit: the pulpy
  centre, the seeds, the hard skin.
- For visual impact, make sure
  all the ingredients can be seen
  in their various contrasting
  layers through the side of
  the glass.
- Mark the difference between
  the crunchy and the soft
  texture as you swallow.

Halve the passion fruit and scoop the pulp into a large
bowl. Add the yogurt and mix them together gently.

Put 2 tablespoonfuls of the honey in the bases of 2
narrow glasses and scatter with half of the hazelnuts.
Spoon half of the yogurt over the nuts and arrange
half of the clementine pieces on top of the yogurt.

Repeat the layering, reserving a few of the nuts for
decoration. Scatter the nuts over the top and chill the
yogurts until you are ready to serve them.

For passion fruit, coconut & strawberry yogurts, soak
2 tablespoons desiccated coconut in 4 tablespoons
skimmed milk for 30 minutes. Mix the passion fruit and
yogurt as above, also folding in the soaked coconut.
Layer as above, omitting the hazelnuts and replacing the
clementines with 100 g (3½ oz) quartered strawberries.

Very berry & fromage frais fool

Calories per serving 219

Serves 4

Preparation time 5 minutes,
 plus cooling and chilling

Cooking time about
 5 minutes

3 tablespoons crème de cassis
 or spiced red fruit cordial
250 g (8 oz) mixed frozen berries
2–4 tablespoons icing sugar, to taste
500 g (1 lb) fat-free fromage frais
250 g (8 oz) low-fat blackcurrant yogurt
1 vanilla pod, split in half lengthways
toasted flaked almonds, to serve

Put the crème de cassis or cordial in a saucepan over
a low heat and gently heat, then add the berries. Stir,
cover and cook for about 5 minutes or until the fruit
has thawed and is beginning to collapse. Remove from
the heat and stir in 1–3 tablespoons of the icing sugar,
according to taste. Leave to cool completely, then chill
for at least 1 hour.

Mix together the fromage frais, yogurt and 1 tablespoon
of the icing sugar in a bowl. Scrape in the seeds from
the vanilla pod and beat to combine. Fold the berries
into the fromage frais mixture until just combined.
Carefully spoon into 4 decorative glasses or glass serving
dishes and serve immediately, scattered with toasted
almonds, if liked.

AWARENESS POINTS

- Taste the berries as you add
  the sugar, stopping at the
  point where they are just
  sweet enough.
- Enjoy the creamy, comforting
  smell of vanilla as you
  scrape the pod and stir the
  fool mixture.
- Think about who you will share
  this with. Offer them a choice
  of toppings, such as muesli
  or nuts.

Apricot tea bread

Calories per serving 230

Cuts into 10

Preparation time 25 minutes, plus soaking

Cooking time 1 hour

100 g (3½ oz) ready-to-eat dried apricots, chopped

100 g (3½ oz) sultanas

100 g (3½ oz) raisins

150 g (5 oz) caster sugar

butter, for greasing and to serve

300 ml (½ pint) hot strong tea

275 g (9 oz) self-raising flour

1 teaspoon bicarbonate of soda

1 teaspoon ground cinnamon

1 egg, beaten

AWARENESS POINTS

- Share this wholesome gift with friends and family to show them your gratitude for the small things they do for you.
- As you add the hot tea, take a moment to inhale the sweet, exotically scented steam.
- Try the bread with salted and unsalted butter, marking the contrast.

Put the dried fruits and sugar in a mixing bowl, add the hot tea and mix together. Leave to soak for 4 hours or overnight.

Grease a 1 kg (2 lb) loaf tin and line its base and 2 long sides with greased nonstick baking paper. Mix the flour, bicarbonate of soda and cinnamon together, add to the soaked fruit with the beaten egg and mix together well.

Spoon into the prepared tin and spread the surface level, then bake in the centre of a preheated oven, 160°C (325°F), Gas Mark 3, for about 1 hour until well risen, the top has cracked and a skewer inserted into the centre comes out clean.

Leave to cool in the tin for 10 minutes, then loosen the edges and lift out of the tin using the lining paper. Transfer to a wire rack, peel off the lining paper and leave to cool completely. Cut into 10 slices and spread with a little butter to serve. This tea bread can be stored, unbuttered, in an airtight tin for up to 1 week.

Granola squares

Calories per serving 399

Makes 12

Preparation time 15 minutes, plus
  chilling

Cooking time 20 minutes

175 g (6 oz) butter, plus extra
  for greasing
150 ml (¼ pint) clear honey
2 tablespoons maple syrup
1 teaspoon ground cinnamon
125 g (4 oz) ready-to-eat dried apricots,
  roughly chopped
100 g (3 ½ oz) ready-to-eat dried papaya
  or mango, roughly chopped
125 g (4 oz) raisins
4 tablespoons pumpkin seeds
2 tablespoons sesame seeds
3 tablespoons sunflower seeds
75 g (3 oz) pecan nuts, roughly chopped
275 g (9 oz) porridge oats

Grease a 28 x 18 cm (11 x 7 inch) deep Swiss roll tin with
butter and line the base with nonstick baking paper.

Place the butter, honey and maple syrup in a medium
saucepan and heat, stirring continually, until the butter
has melted. Add the cinnamon, dried fruit, seeds and
nuts, stir the mixture and heat for 1 minute. Remove
from the heat and add the porridge oats, stirring until
they are well coated in the syrup.

Transfer the mixture to the prepared tin and smooth
down with the back of a spoon to compact into the
tin and level. Bake in a preheated oven, 180°C (350°F),
Gas Mark 4, for 15 minutes until the top is just
beginning to brown. Leave to cool in the tin, then chill
in the refrigerator for 30–60 minutes.

Turn out the chilled granola, upside down, on a
chopping board, then carefully flip it back over to its
correct side. Using a long, sharp knife (preferably longer
than the granola itself), cut into 12 squares.

AWARENESS POINTS

- Taste the dried ingredients –
  are they sweet, chewy, hard
  or bitter?
- Enjoy the aroma of butter,
  honey and syrup warming
  in the pan as it suffuses
  your kitchen.
- See whether you can taste
  the individual nuts and seeds
  in the granola – is the sesame
  there, and can you detect
  the cinnamon?

Mango & vanilla muffin slice

Calories per serving 336

Cuts into 8

Preparation time 20 minutes

Cooking time 1 hour

100 g (3½ oz) slightly salted butter, melted, plus extra for greasing

1 small ripe mango

225 g (7½ oz) plain flour

2 teaspoons baking powder

150 g (5 oz) golden caster sugar

50 g (2 oz) porridge oats

1 egg, beaten

175 ml (6 fl oz) milk

1 teaspoon vanilla bean paste or extract

vanilla sugar, for sprinkling

AWARENESS POINTS

- Enjoy the methodical, careful process of cutting a mango.
- Notice the homely smell of baking and how it differs with the addition of exotic mango.
- Serve with your favourite tea, brewed just to your liking.

Grease a 1 kg (2 lb) loaf tin with butter and line with nonstick baking paper.

Halve the mango each side of the flat central stone. Cut away the stone, then peel and dice the flesh into 5 mm (¼ inch) pieces.

Sift the flour and baking powder into a bowl, then stir in the caster sugar and oats. Beat together the egg, milk, vanilla and melted butter in a jug. Add to the dry ingredients with half the mango and stir together using a large metal spoon until just combined.

Spoon the mixture into the prepared tin and scatter with the remaining mango pieces. Bake in a preheated oven, 180°C (350°F), Gas Mark 4, for about 1 hour or until well risen, firm to the touch and a skewer inserted into the centre comes out clean.

Leave to cool in the tin for 5 minutes, then loosen at the ends and transfer to a wire rack to cool. Peel off the lining paper and serve warm or cold, sprinkled with vanilla sugar.

Lunch

Moving with a mindful mind

Mindful movement can be a way of getting you off the couch, so that you can start enjoying simple activities such as walking again. But the 'mindfulness' factor can also be an important addition to an existing workout routine.

Mindful movement

The mindful form of exercise brings you back in touch with your body through movement. The founding father of mindfulness within the secular world, Jon Kabat-Zinn, introduced yoga into his programme because he had found it to be enjoyable in his own life. As he said in 1990, 'The focus is on maintaining moment-to-moment awareness of the sensations accompanying our movements, letting go of any thoughts or feelings about the sensations themselves.' Mindfulness flourishes under what are called the eight attitudinal foundations of mindfulness. Knowing them will help you to differentiate between a normal practice and a mindful movement practice.

The eight attitudinal foundations are:
    Non-judging
    Patience
    Beginner's mind (childlike curiosity)
    Trust
    Non-striving
    Acceptance
    Letting go

If your exercise teacher (and remember you are your own teacher when you practise at home) enables you to integrate these elements into your movement practice, you are on the right track.

In fact any activity done with a mindful attitude can help you to get through the day with ease, calm and enough energy to keep going. On top of that you can discover gifts of tranquillity and focus you thought you could never have. Encourage yourself to engage in a movement practice you really like (how about dancing!?) and it can help you to relieve the stress that has been stored in your body. Mindful movement can bring you a feeling of coming home, to the here and now, through self-acceptance, awareness and kindness.

A short yoga practice

Free up the neck: sit on a chair, looking ahead, then allow the chin to drop onto the breast bone. Then look up again. Repeat a few times and be very mindful of the movement that occurs in your neck/cervical spine. Come back to the start position and feel the neck now.

Sit upright, look ahead and allow the head to drop forward onto the chest. Now gently let the head sway left and right in small movements like a pendulum. Follow the movement attentively. When you have repeated it 5–7 times come back to the upright position and feel the neck now.

Free up the shoulders: you can do this movement sitting, lying down or even in the morning before you get out of bed. With the arms along the sides of the body, draw the right shoulder up towards the ear and let it sink back to the start position. Repeat several times, then stop and sense into the upper body and shoulder. Then draw the right shoulder forwards and back. Repeat several times and come back to the start position. Feel the upper body and shoulder now. Then bring these two movements together and start to circle the right shoulder. When you have finished, compare the right side with the left. Do you notice any difference? In size, temperature, weight, length? Now repeat on the other side and then circle both shoulders together.

Mindful walking

Most of us can engage in a practical exercise such as walking. It is safe, doesn't cost anything and with proper clothing can be done anytime and anywhere. It can be done whether you are old or young, stiff or mobile, healthy and fit or recovering from illness and exhaustion. Walking can accommodate each one of us, whoever we are, whatever condition we are in. It has many health benefits, as it conditions the heart and lungs, burns calories and helps to de-stress by expelling stale air from the lungs. The goal is not to reach any destination but to develop understanding and awareness of the sensations that occur in the body while you are walking.

Become aware of the muscles and the joints in your body as you move. Start with some slow steps and notice how your foot makes contact with the ground. Then pay attention to the lifting of the heel and the push-off from the toes, the weight distribution on your foot, the engagement of your calf muscles and hamstrings, and the ankle, knee and hip joints. Notice your trunk swaying and your arms swinging. Start to playfully increase your speed, but remember, it is not about reaching any destination: your goal is awareness of the body moving.

Scan your body from head to toes for any unnecessary tension. Be aware of the areas around the neck, shoulders and lower back. Ask yourself what is needed to make this movement light and enjoyable.Lengthen your stride and as you do so see if your arms can swing a bit further. Try to lead the movement from your pelvis and navel centre, rather than from your head or chest. Walk for at least 10 minutes and then gradually reduce your pace.

Guided practice

1 After any activity, your energy levels need restoring. Energy comes from carbohydrates and while some of these should be eaten in moderation, plenty of others are extremely healthy and can be eaten as part of a mindful diet. Protein is also essential for healthy, strong muscles, and it helps you to feel full for longer.

2 The recipes in this section have been chosen to provide you with the right sort of energy and balanced nutrition for an active lifestyle. It is important to balance movement with rest. Your lung capacity improves with exercise. The freeness of breath, exhilaration and release of endorphins produce a fantastic rush, but it is important to take the time to enjoy this as well as to contrast the experience with calm and stillness. Return to slow breathing and find the stillness and peace required for mindful eating.

3 This first recipe here is quick, easy and versatile – excellent for those with a busy, active lifestyle. Salmon is great source of protein and essential oils. Its vibrant colour is always a delight to look at and as the bright red warms to a delicate pink, you can appreciate every stage of the cooking process. Bulghar wheat is rich in protein and minerals and has a nutty taste. It provides an excellent contrast to the flaky, oily salmon and crisp green vegetables.

4 As you eat, notice how your body receives the food. Let it reward your movement and restore your energy levels. Remember to eat slowly, returning the body and breath to a state of stillness and peace. It is common for people who have exercised to overeat and treat food as a reward, so remember to pause frequently and really listen to your body's fullness signals.

5 In particular, the zingy lemon will bring out the light flavour of the salmon. Appreciate how fresh that feels with the green vegetables. Imagine every mouthful is helping to restore your body. Take time to appreciate how energized and satisfied you feel.

Salmon & bulgar wheat pilaf

Calories per serving 478
Serves 4
Preparation time 10 minutes
Cooking time 10—15 minutes

475 g (15 oz) boneless, skinless salmon
250 g (8 oz) bulgar wheat
75 g (3 oz) frozen peas
200 g (7 oz) runner beans, chopped
2 tablespoons chopped chives
2 tablespoons chopped flat leaf parsley
salt and pepper

To serve
2 lemons, halved
low-fat yogurt

Cook the salmon in a steamer or microwave for about 10 minutes. Alternatively, wrap it in foil and cook in a preheated oven, 180°C (350°F), Gas Mark 4, for 15 minutes.

Meanwhile, cook the bulgar wheat according to the instructions on the packet and boil the peas and beans. Alternatively, cook the bulgar wheat, peas and beans in the steamer with the salmon.

Flake the salmon and mix it into the bulgar wheat with the peas and beans. Fold in the chives and parsley and season to taste. Serve immediately with lemon halves and yogurt.

Cream of leek & pea soup

Calories per serving 322

Serves 4

Preparation time 15 minutes

Cooking time 25 minutes

2 tablespoons olive oil

375 g (12 oz) leeks, trimmed, cleaned
  and thinly sliced

375 g (12 oz) fresh shelled
  or frozen peas

900 ml (1½ pints) vegetable stock

1 small bunch of mint

150 g (5 oz) full-fat mascarpone cheese

grated rind of 1 small lemon

salt and pepper

To garnish (optional)

mint leaves

lemon rind curls

Heat the oil in a saucepan, add the leeks and toss
in the oil, then cover and fry gently for 10 minutes,
stirring occasionally, until softened but not coloured.
Mix in the peas and cook briefly.

Pour the stock into the pan, add a little salt and pepper,
then bring to the boil. Cover and simmer gently for
10 minutes. Ladle half the soup into a blender or food
processor, add the mint and blend until smooth.
Pour the purée back into the saucepan.

Mix the mascarpone with half the lemon rind, reserving
the rest for a garnish. Spoon half the mixture into the
soup, then reheat, stirring until the mascarpone has
melted. Taste and adjust the seasoning if needed. Ladle
the soup into 4 warmed bowls, top with spoonfuls of
the remaining mascarpone and a sprinkling of the
remaining lemon rind. Garnish with mint leaves and
lemon rind curls, if liked.

AWARENESS POINTS

- Shelling peas is a repetitive
  task so why not sit somewhere
  relaxing or listen to music
  as you do it.
- Enjoy the vivid, bright green
  colours. Smell the mint
  leaves and lemon rind curls
  – appreciate the freshness
  and note down any emotions.
  Perhaps it makes you think
  of the outdoors.
- Serve in your favourite bowl,
  taking the time to garnish
  the soup so it looks impressive
  and reflects your efforts.

Fruity stuffed peppers

Calories per serving 421

Serves 4

Preparation time 15 minutes

Cooking time 1 hour

2 red peppers, cored, deseeded and
  halved

2 orange peppers, cored, deseeded
  and halved

2 tablespoons olive oil, plus extra
  for brushing

1 red onion, chopped

1 garlic clove, crushed

1 small red chilli, deseeded
  and finely chopped

25 g (1 oz) pine nuts

200 g (7 oz) cooked wild rice

400 g (13 oz) can green lentils, rinsed
  and drained

250 g (8 oz) cherry tomatoes, quartered

100 g (3½ oz) ready-to-eat dried
  apricots, chopped

handful of sultanas

grated rind of 1 lemon

2 tablespoons chopped fresh herbs

100 g (3½ oz) feta cheese, crumbled

AWARENESS POINTS

- Notice the fresh, bittersweet
  smell as you prepare the peppers.
- Take a small mouthful and
  chew slowly, noticing the
  different tastes and textures.
- Which is your favourite
  combination?

Put the peppers in an ovenproof dish, cut-side up, and
brush each with a little oil. Place in a preheated oven,
200°C (400°F), Gas Mark 6, for 20 minutes.

Meanwhile, heat the oil in frying pan, add the onion,
garlic and chilli and fry for 2 minutes, then add the
pine nuts and cook for a further 2 minutes until golden.
Stir in all the remaining ingredients.

Remove the peppers from the oven and spoon the
stuffing mixture into the peppers. Cover with foil,
return to the oven and cook for 25 minutes, then
remove the foil and cook for a further 15 minutes.
Serve with a crisp salad.

Hot & sour soup

Calories per serving 161

Serves 4

Preparation time 10 minutes

Cooking time 12 minutes

750 ml (1¼ pints) vegetable or fish stock

4 dried kaffir lime leaves

2.5 cm (1 inch) piece of fresh root
   ginger, peeled and grated

1 red chilli, deseeded and sliced

1 lemon grass stalk, lightly bruised

125 g (4 oz) mushrooms, sliced

100 g (3½ oz) rice noodles

75 g (3 oz) baby spinach leaves

125 g (4 oz) cooked, peeled tiger prawns,
   or defrosted if frozen, rinsed with
   cold water and drained

2 tablespoons lemon juice

black pepper

AWARENESS POINTS

- Feel the different hard and soft
  textures you are preparing.
- Consider the smell of lemon
  grass. Does it seem savoury
  or sweet?
- Note the riot of colours and
  shapes in this dish.

Put the stock, lime leaves, fresh root ginger, chilli and lemon grass in a large saucepan. Cover and bring to the boil. Add the mushrooms and simmer for 2 minutes. Break the noodles into short lengths, drop into the soup and simmer for 3 minutes.

Add the baby spinach and prawns and simmer for 2 minutes until the prawns are heated through. Add the lemon juice. Remove and discard the lemon grass stalk and season the soup with black pepper before serving.

Chicken minestrone

Calories per serving 197
Serves 4
Preparation time 5 minutes
Cooking time 10 minutes

400 g (13 oz) can chopped tomatoes
600 ml (1 pint) chicken stock
125 g (4 oz) cooked chicken, chopped
1 courgette, chopped
125 g (4 oz) mixed frozen vegetables
70 g (2½ oz) mini-pasta shapes
1 tablespoon ready-made pesto
salt and pepper

AWARENESS POINTS

- Choose fun or colourful pasta shapes.
- Notice the smell of the soup and any memories it evokes for you.
- Vary your choice of vegetables for nutrition and flavour.

Put the tomatoes, stock, chicken, courgette and frozen vegetables in a saucepan. Bring to the boil, stirring, then add the pasta shapes and simmer for 5 minutes until the pasta is just tender.

Season with salt and pepper and stir in the pesto just before serving.

For vegetable chicken & rice, put a 400 g (13 oz) can chopped tomatoes in a saucepan with 200 g (7 oz) chopped cooked chicken, 1 chopped courgette, 125 g (4 oz) frozen mixed vegetables and 125 ml (4 fl oz) chicken stock and heat. Simmer for 5 minutes, add 250 g (8 oz) long grain rice and simmer for a further 10 minutes, stirring occasionally, or until the rice is cooked, adding a little boiling water if the mixture is too dry. Stir in 125 g (4 oz) baby spinach leaves until just wilted.

Fig, bean & toasted pecan salad

Calories per serving 352

Serves 4

Preparation time 5 minutes,
   plus cooling

Cooking time 5–6 minutes

100 g (3½ oz) pecan nuts

200 g (7 oz) green beans, trimmed

4 fresh figs, cut into quarters

100 g (3½ oz) rocket leaves

small handful of mint leaves

50 g (2 oz) Parmesan or pecorino cheese

Dressing

3 tablespoons walnut oil

2 teaspoons sherry vinegar

1 teaspoon vincotto or balsamic vinegar

salt and pepper

Heat a heavy-based frying pan over a medium heat, add the pecans and dry-fry for 3–4 minutes, stirring frequently, until browned. Tip onto a small plate and leave to cool.

Cook the beans in a saucepan of lightly salted boiling water for 2 minutes. Drain, refresh under cold running water and pat dry with kitchen paper. Put the beans in a bowl with the figs, pecans, rocket and mint.

Whisk together all the dressing ingredients in a small bowl and season with salt and pepper. Pour over the salad and toss well. Shave over the Parmesan or pecorino and serve.

AWARENESS POINTS

- Have you grown your own beans or mint? If you can, pick a fresh mint leaf, and rub it between your fingers. What do you notice?

- Do the raisin experience (see page 18), but using a fig quarter. Do you notice a sinewy texture? What are its three main characteristics?

- Why not sample different vinegars and oil? A local farmers' market is a great place to do this. You could do the same with cheeses – get to know your favourites.

Warm chicken & pine nut salad

Calories per serving 319

Serves 4

Preparation time 10 minutes

Cooking time 15 minutes

4 tablespoons pine nuts

4 boneless, skinless chicken breasts, halved horizontally

2–3 teaspoons paprika

1 tablespoon olive oil

handful of radicchio leaves

100 g (3½ oz) mixed salad leaves

1 red onion, thinly sliced

4 tablespoons sherry vinegar

2 teaspoons Dijon mustard

2 tablespoons clear honey

50 g (2 oz) raisins

salt and pepper

AWARENESS POINTS

- Taste a pine nut before you cook – notice the buttery, soft texture inside.
- How does radicchio compare in taste to the other salad leaves?
- Mark the contrast of warm dressing and cold salad.

Heat a nonstick frying pan until hot. Add the pine nuts and dry-fry, stirring continuously, until golden, taking care not to let them burn. Tip them out of the pan on to a plate.

Lightly dust the chicken breast halves with paprika and season with salt and pepper. Heat the oil in the pan and fry the chicken breasts for about 10 minutes, turning occasionally, or until cooked through.

Meanwhile, mix together the radicchio, salad leaves and red onion and divide among 4 serving plates. Remove the chicken from the pan and stir the vinegar, mustard and honey into the pan juices. Heat through and add the raisins and pine nuts. Top the salad with the chicken pieaces, then pour the warm dressing over the salad and serve.

Rocket, *pear* & pecorino salad

Calories per serving 195

Serves 4

Preparation time 10 minutes

250 g (8 oz) rocket leaves
2 pears, quartered and cored
75 g (3 oz) pecorino cheese shavings

Dressing
1 teaspoon Dijon mustard
2 tablespoons cider vinegar
2 tablespoons olive oil
salt and pepper

AWARENESS POINTS

- Notice the peppery taste of the rocket.
- How does it change the flavour of the pears?
- Think about what size fruit slices will work best for flavour and presentation.

Make the dressing. Whisk together the mustard, cider vinegar and oil. Season to taste with salt and pepper.

Put the rocket in a large salad bowl. Finely slice the pears and add them to the rocket. Add the dressing to the salad and toss carefully to mix.

Layer most of the pecorino shavings through the rocket and pear salad, garnish with the remaining shavings and serve.

For rocket, apple & balsamic salad, combine 250 g (8 oz) rocket leaves, 1 finely sliced green apple and 75 g (3 oz) pecorino cheese shavings in a large salad bowl. Whisk together 2 tablespoons aged balsamic vinegar and 3 tablespoons olive oil. Add the dressing to the salad, toss carefully to mix and serve immediately.

Guided practice

Part of Mindful cooking is to experiment with flavours and use your intuition. Listen to your body and adapt the recipe to suit your needs. As with many of the salads in this chapter, you can apply basic nutrition and swap ingredients for your choice of protein, fruit, vegetables, nuts and seeds.

1 Celery has a high water content. After cutting, take a bite-size amount and notice how the water explodes in your mouth as you slowly chew. What noise does it make, what is the texture? Do the same with the apricots and the almonds. Can you rate their textures from smooth to wrinkled, soft to hard, chewy to brittle?

2 Salads should never feel dull or boring so garnish this dish like it is a work of art. Make sure your plate looks full of food you are tempted to eat. Try and get all the elements of the salad on to the fork and savour all the flavours at once. Chew each mouthful 20–30 times and then put the fork down. Take a breath. Imagine you are at the height of your day, your energy levels are at their peak, your body needs to feel strong and lively.

3 Finally, make sure you take a full lunch hour and get a change of scenery. Take the time to notice how you feel after your lunch. Have you had time to digest? Have you eaten just the right amount so that you don't feel uncomfortable and lethargic?

Chicken & apricot salad

Calories per serving 366
Serves 4
Preparation time 15 minutes

200 g (7 oz) celery
75 g (3 oz) almonds, roughly chopped
3 tablespoons chopped parsley
4 tablespoons mayonnaise
3 poached or roasted chicken breasts,
   each about 150 g (5 oz), shredded
12 fresh apricots, halved and stoned
salt and pepper

Thinly slice the celery sticks diagonally,
reserving the yellow inner leaves. Transfer
to a large salad bowl together with half
the leaves. Add half the almonds to the bowl
with the parsley and mayonnaise. Season
to taste with salt and pepper.

Arrange the salad on a serving plate.
Add the chicken and apricots to the salad
and stir lightly to combine.

Garnish with the remaining almonds
and celery leaves and serve.

Beetroot, spinach & orange salad

Calories per serving 221

Serves 4

Preparation time 20 minutes, plus cooling

Cooking time 1–2 hours

500 g (1 lb) uncooked beetroots, preferably of a similar size

2 garlic cloves, peeled and left whole

handful of oregano leaves

1 teaspoon vegetable oil

1 tablespoon balsamic vinegar

200 g (7 oz) baby spinach leaves

2 oranges, peeled, white pith removed and cut into segments

salt and pepper

Vinaigrette

1 tablespoon balsamic vinegar

1 teaspoon Dijon mustard

4 tablespoons olive oil

pinch of sugar (optional)

Put the whole beetroots in the centre of a large piece of foil, along with the garlic and oregano. Sprinkle with pepper and drizzle over the vegetable oil and vinegar. Gather up the foil loosely and fold over at the top to seal it. Place on a baking sheet and bake in a preheated oven, 200°C (400°F), Gas Mark 6, for 1–2 hours (depending on how large the beetroots are) until tender. Unwrap the foil parcel and leave the beetroots to cool before peeling and slicing them. Discard the garlic.

Make the vinaigrette. Mix together the balsamic vinegar and mustard in a small bowl. Season with a little salt and pepper. Gradually add the olive oil, whisking constantly, until smooth and well combined. Taste and adjust the seasoning as needed, adding a pinch of sugar to reduce the acidity, if liked, bearing in mind the sweetness of the roasted beetroots. Whisk again until the sugar has dissolved. Alternatively, put all the vinaigrette ingredients in a screw-top jar, seal tightly and shake vigorously until well combined.

Put the spinach in a large bowl, then gently toss together with the beetroots and oranges. Drizzle over the vinaigrette and sprinkle with pepper.

AWARENESS POINTS

- Buy local or organic beetroots if you can.
- Take time to appreciate the smell of roasting garlic and oregano.
- Enjoy the contrast of earthy beetroot with sharp vinaigrette and sweet orange.

Prawns with black sesame seeds

Calories per serving 132
Serves 4 (with 2 other main dishes)
Preparation time 10 minutes
Cooking time about 10 minutes

½ tablespoon black sesame seeds

1½ tablespoons sunflower oil

2–3 garlic cloves, finely chopped

250 g (8 oz) raw prawns, peeled and
  deveined, with tails left intact

200 g (7 oz) water chestnuts, drained
  and thinly sliced

125 g (4 oz) mangetout, trimmed

2 tablespoons vegetable stock, seafood
  stock or water

1 tablespoon light soy sauce

1 tablespoon oyster sauce

AWARENESS POINTS
- Be aware of the fragrance of
  the seeds as you cook them.
- Note the changing colours of
  the garlic and the prawns.
- Mark the fresh crunchiness
  of the mangetout and water
  chestnuts.

Dry-fry the black sesame seeds in a small pan for
1–2 minutes or until fragrant, then set aside.

Heat the oil in a wok or large frying pan and stir-fry
the garlic over a medium heat until it is lightly browned.

Add the prawns, water chestnuts and mangetout and
stir-fry over a high heat for 1–2 minutes. Add the stock,
soy sauce and oyster sauce and stir-fry for a further
2–3 minutes or until the prawns open and turn pink.
Stir in the fried sesame seeds and serve immediately.

Aromatic chicken pancakes

Calories per serving 269

Serves 4

Preparation time 10 minutes

Cooking time 7 minutes

4 boneless, skinless chicken breasts,
   about 150 g (5 oz) each
6 tablespoons hoisin sauce

To serve

12 Chinese pancakes, warmed
½ cucumber, cut into matchsticks
12 spring onions, thinly sliced
handful of fresh coriander
4 tablespoons hoisin sauce mixed
   with 3 tablespoons water

AWARENESS POINTS

- Chop the spring onions and cucumber into long, thin strips to echo their natural shapes. Notice how delicate and light the matchstick vegetables feel.

- Smell and taste the hoisin sauce. Can you detect soy, chillies or garlic? Notice how the sweet and salty sauce highlights the savoury duck flavour.

- This meal is great to share and allows others to get involved. Encourage people to assemble and wrap their own pancakes. Note how people's tastes vary.

Lay a chicken breast between 2 sheets of clingfilm and flatten with a rolling pin or meat mallet until it is 2.5 cm (1 inch) thick. Repeat with the remaining chicken breasts. Transfer to a baking sheet and brush with some of the hoisin sauce.

Cook the chicken breasts under a preheated hot grill for 4 minutes. Turn them over, brush with the remaining hoisin sauce and cook for a further 3 minutes or until the chicken is cooked through.

Meanwhile, warm the pancakes in a bamboo steamer for 3 minutes or until heated through.

Slice the chicken thinly and arrange it on a serving plate. Serve with the pancakes, accompanied by the cucumber, spring onions, coriander and diluted hoisin sauce in separate bowls, so that everyone can assemble their own pancakes.

Greek country salad with haloumi

Calories per serving 398

Serves 4

Preparation time 10 minutes

Cooking time 2 minutes

4 vine-ripened tomatoes, roughly
  chopped

½ onion, sliced

1 Lebanese cucumber,
  thickly sliced

100 g (3½ oz) pitted black Kalamata
  olives

1 small cos lettuce

250 g (8 oz) haloumi cheese, sliced

Dressing

4 tablespoons extra-virgin olive oil

1½ tablespoons red wine vinegar

1 teaspoon dried oregano

salt and pepper

AWARENESS POINTS

- Do you know what types of
  olives you like? Take the time
  to sample different types.
- Enjoy the bright colours as you
  combine the ingredients.
- Notice how the flavours of
  oregano and halloumi enhance
  one another.

Put the tomatoes, onion, cucumber and olives in a bowl.
Tear the lettuce into pieces and add to the salad. Toss
well and arrange on a large platter.

Whisk all the dressing ingredients together in a small
bowl and season with salt and pepper. Drizzle a little
over the salad.

Heat a heavy-based frying pan until hot, add the
haloumi slices and cook for 1 minute on each side until
they are charred and softened. Arrange on top of the
salad, drizzle over the remaining dressing and serve.

For Greek salad with chunky croûtons, replace the
haloumi with 200 g (7 oz) crumbled feta cheese. To
make the croûtons, cut thick slices of close-textured
country bread, then cut these into large chunks. Heat a
little olive oil in a frying pan and fry the bread, turning
occasionally, until crisp and golden. Add extra olive oil
as needed. Cool, then toss into the salad and serve.

Lime & coconut squid

Calories per serving 452
Serves 2
Preparation time 15 minutes
Cooking time 5 minutes

10–12 prepared baby squid, about 375 g
   (12 oz) including tentacles, cleaned
4 limes, halved

Dressing
2 red chillies, deseeded and finely
   chopped
finely grated rind and juice of 2 limes
2.5 cm (1 inch) piece of fresh root
   ginger, peeled and grated
100 g (3½ oz) freshly grated coconut
4 tablespoons groundnut oil
1–2 tablespoons chilli oil
1 tablespoon white wine vinegar

Cut down the side of each squid so that they can be laid flat on a chopping board. Using a sharp knife, lightly score the inside flesh in a crisscross pattern.

Mix all the dressing ingredients together in a bowl. Toss the squid in half the dressing until thoroughly coated.

Heat a ridged griddle pan until smoking hot, add the limes, cut side down, and cook for 2 minutes or until well charred. Remove from the pan and set aside. Keeping the griddle pan very hot, add the squid pieces and cook for 1 minute. Turn them over and cook for a further minute or until they turn white, lose their transparency and are charred.

Transfer the squid to a chopping board and cut into strips. Drizzle with the remaining dressing and serve immediately with the charred limes and a salad of mixed green leaves.

AWARENESS POINTS
- Source your seafood with care, and buy ethically.
- As you grate the ginger, notice the spicy, sweet smell.
- Enjoy the contrast of the charred, sweet/sour limes with the spicy dressing.

Seared chicken sandwiches

Calories per serving 293
Serves 4
Preparation time 15 minutes
Cooking time 5–6 minutes

250 g (8 oz) mini chicken breasts
8 teaspoons balsamic vinegar
8 slices of granary bread
6 tablespoons low-fat natural yogurt
½–1 teaspoon freshly grated hot
  horseradish or horseradish sauce,
  to taste
100 g (3½ oz) mixed salad leaves with
  beetroot strips
pepper

AWARENESS POINTS

- Sample a tiny drop of balsamic vinegar, noticing its thick texture and sweetness.
- Mixing the yogurt with horseradish, taste frequently and notice how the heat increases.
- Layer the sandwich ingredients carefully to present their colours.

Put the mini chicken breasts into a plastic bag with half the vinegar and toss together until evenly coated.

Heat a nonstick frying pan, lift the chicken out of the plastic bag with a fork and add the pieces to the pan. Fry for 3 minutes, turn and drizzle with the vinegar from the bag and cook for a further 2–3 minutes or until browned and cooked through.

Toast the bread lightly on both sides. Slice the chicken into long, thin strips. Mix together the yogurt and horseradish and a little pepper to taste. Add the salad leaves and toss together.

Arrange the yogurt and salad leaves on 4 slices of toast, then add some chicken strips, drizzle over the remaining vinegar, if liked, and top with the remaining slices of toast. Cut each sandwich in half and serve immediately.

For tangy chicken, lemon & garlic toasties, toss the chicken fillets with the juice of ½ lemon and 1 tablespoon olive oil, then fry as above omitting the vinegar. Toast 8 slices of wholemeal bread, then spread with 4 tablespoons reduced-fat garlic mayonnaise. Divide the chicken between 4 slices of toast then top with the shredded leaves of 2 Little Gem lettuces and a 5 cm (2 inch) piece of cucumber, thinly sliced. Cover with the remaining slices of toast, then press together and cut into triangles.

Griddled vegetable platter

Calories per serving 285
  (not including bread)

Serves 4

Preparation time 10 minutes,
  plus marinating

Cooking time 20–30 minutes

2 courgettes, sliced lengthways into
  5 mm (¼ inch) thick slices

1 aubergine, sliced lengthways into
  5 mm (¼ inch) thick slices

1 yellow pepper, cored, deseeded and
  cut into 2.5 cm (1 inch) thick slices

1 red pepper, cored, deseeded and cut
  into 2.5 cm (1 inch) thick slices

100 ml (3½ fl oz) extra-virgin olive oil

2 garlic cloves, crushed

large pinch of crushed dried chillies

handful of small mint and/or basil
  leaves

salt

Toss all the prepared vegetables in 2 tablespoons of the oil until well coated.

Heat a ridged griddle pan over a high heat until smoking hot. Add the courgettes and aubergine in batches and cook for 2–3 minutes on each side. Transfer to a bowl and toss with the remaining oil, the garlic and crushed dried chillies. Set aside.

Add the peppers in batches to the reheated griddle pan and cook for 3–4 minutes on each side, then combine with the courgettes and aubergine. Season with salt and toss in the herbs.

Cover and leave to marinate at room temperature for 30 minutes. Serve with slices of country bread, if liked.

AWARENESS POINTS

- Vary the vegetables according to season and local availability.
- Enjoy the sound, smells and heat as they sizzle.
- Arrange the vegetables creatively so that their bright colours stand out.

Teriyaki chicken with three seeds

Calories per serving 307

Serves 4

Preparation time 20 minutes, plus marinating

Cooking time 20–30 minutes

4 boneless, skinless chicken breasts, about 125 g (4 oz) each

2 tablespoons sunflower oil

4 tablespoons soy sauce

2 garlic cloves, finely chopped

2.5 cm (1 inch) piece of fresh root ginger, peeled and finely grated

2 tablespoons sesame seeds

2 tablespoons sunflower seeds

2 tablespoons pumpkin seeds

juice of 2 limes

100 g (3½ oz) herb salad

½ small iceberg lettuce, torn into bite-sized pieces

50 g (2 oz) alfalfa or broccoli sprouting seeds

AWARENESS POINTS

- Slowly chew each kind of seed and notice their different tastes.
- Smell the garlic and ginger as they combine and cook.
- As you arrange the vegetables, mark the contrasting shades of green.

Put the chicken breasts into a shallow china dish. Spoon three-quarters of the oil over the chicken, then add half the soy sauce, the garlic and the ginger.

Turn the chicken to coat in the mixture, then leave to marinate for 30 minutes.

Heat a nonstick frying pan, then lift the chicken out of the marinade and add to the pan. Fry for 8–10 minutes on each side until dark brown and cooked all the way through. Lift out and set aside.

Heat the remaining oil in the pan, add the seeds and fry for 2–3 minutes until lightly toasted. Add the remaining marinade and remaining soy sauce, bring to the boil, then take off the heat and mix in the lime juice.

Mix the herb salad, lettuce and sprouting seeds together, then spoon over 4 serving plates. Thinly slice the chicken and arrange on top, then spoon the seed and lime dressing over the top. Serve immediately.

Dinner

Making food from scratch

When we entertain friends and family for a special occasion, we tend to put in extra time and effort and prepare food ourselves rather than buying ready-made food. It becomes a ritual of sorts and can give us a heightened sense of wellbeing. Now is the time to expand your thoughts about eating to include the wider community and the world. Where food comes from, and to whom it goes, is an essential part of mindful eating. The more we step back from the complex processes that food-production companies employ, the more we are able to appreciate that simple food can soothe the soul.

Making food from scratch can be a rewarding pastime, as well as a reward when you sit down and eat it!

Enjoy your bread

You may wonder what freshly baked bread has to do with mindful eating. Let me explain. By baking your own bread, even if you do it just once in a while, you will explore another aspect of what it means to live a mindful life. Making progress in practising mindfulness by taking small steps encourages you to trust the process. Hopefully you have found some of the ideas and recipes in this book to be healing and nourishing, and to a certain extent, that is what can be said of making bread. When we make our own bread, we engage in a process that seeks integrity. It requires time and patience, and reminds us that good things unfold slowly, in their own time. It reminds us that less can be more – less noise in our head, more calm instead. This is so true in relation to bread.

How to eat well without causing suffering to others

- Buy from local farmers.
- Use canvas bags for your shopping and refuse plastic ones.
- Eat produce that is in season and has not been flown from distant places. You will reduce your carbon footprint.
- If you must eat meat, choose organic and free-range.
- How about some mindful gardening? Grow your own herbs, fruit and vegetables.
- Make your own jams and chutneys, from your home-grown products if possible – good for you and your family, and good as gifts for others.

Making connections

Some of us feel that something is missing from our lives and we tend to try to fill this emptiness with food.

If you ask yourself what you are really longing for and what it is that brings you true happiness, what would you answer? Many people say that they want to live together in peace, free from torture and war. To live in a world where there is enough for all to share, and to protect the beauty of the planet. But when we look at the daily news another picture emerges.

In our so-called civilized society, we have to face up to leaders who seem to care more about what is best for them rather than for the whole of society, and who live with greed, dishonesty and corruption.

We can't change them, but we can make small changes in our own lives. One way to do this is by eating together. How many families eat their meals separately? Sharing a meal with others can truly enrich your life. By cooking and eating together, even just for an evening, you can create a community that has values, such as not turning away strangers in need for food.

Conclusion

The food we eat and the food we buy matters. By being mindful, we build connections with others and make better choices. We understand what we really want. Mindfulness encourages us to enjoy the food in front of us, simple or rich, whether alone or with others, and reminds us that this is the first step. Try to go deeper and discover the inner nourishment of feeling your human connectedness and you will become less self-centred and more open. If you can achieve this, you will change your eating habits because you will know the impact you are having on others.

More ideas

It's not just baking bread that brings a happiness reward. Baking other food is a great way to spend an afternoon or weekend. From batches of scones to trays of cupcakes, you can chart the mindful journey it takes you on. Making jam is a great way to use home-grown fruit and to recycle jars (be sure to sterilize them first), and batch cooking can be great for busy professionals. Cook a hearty soup or stew that can be kept or frozen, so you can quickly heat up a healthy meal after work.

Guided practice

A perfect roast meal will bring friends and family together. When you cook this recipe, spend some time thinking about what you are really trying to achieve – is it the perfect cooking result, or meaningful time spent with loved ones? Perhaps it is a celebration, or an anniversary, or the opportunity to catch up with someone you haven't seen in a long time.

1 Keep these thoughts in your head as you go about preparing the lamb – the ritual of stuffing and securing with skewers. Focus on the colour – tiny specks of tomatoes, wild rice and parsley – how do they light up the meat and add a sense of occasion?

2 Artichoke hearts are a delicacy so take the time to study their unusual shape and texture. Look and compare each layer. How do the intricate centres compare to the rough exterior? As the roast begins to cook, do you feel a sense of familiarity and comfort? What memories does it evoke? Do they give off an aroma?

3 In a relaxed atmosphere with others, we often eat more than we really need. To avoid this, start eating only when everyone else at the table has begun. This will help you to slow down from the outset. Listen more and talk less, so you can concentrate on eating slowly. Tune in with another person who eats slowly. Follow his or her speed. Enjoy more and eat less.

Lamb stuffed with rice & peppers

Calories per serving 412
(not including roast potatoes)
Serves 4
Preparation time 40 minutes
Cooking time 1 hour 20 minutes

2 red peppers, cored, deseeded and halved
50 g (2 oz) wild rice, cooked
5 garlic cloves, chopped
5 semi-dried tomatoes, chopped
2 tablespoons chopped flat leaf parsley
625 g (1¼ lb) boneless leg of lamb, butterflied
4 artichoke halves
salt and pepper

Put the pepper halves in a roasting tin and cook in a preheated oven, 180°C (350°F), Gas Mark 4, for 20 minutes until the skin has blackened and blistered. Cover with damp kitchen paper and set aside. When the peppers are cool enough to handle, peel off the skin and chop the flesh. (Leave the oven on.)

Mix together 1 of the chopped peppers, the rice, garlic, tomatoes and parsley. Season to taste.

Put the lamb on a board and make a horizontal incision, almost all the way along, to make a cavity for stuffing. Fold back the top half, spoon in the stuffing and fold back the top. Secure with skewers. Cook the lamb for 1 hour, basting frequently and adding the artichokes and other pepper for the last 15 minutes of cooking time. Slice the lamb and serve immediately with roasted new potatoes, if liked.

Oriental chicken cakes

Calories per serving 213
   (not including rice noodle salad)
Serves 4
Preparation time 15 minutes
Cooking time 16 minutes

575 g (1 lb 3 oz) minced chicken
1 lemon grass stalk, very finely chopped
2 kaffir lime leaves, very finely chopped
5 cm (2 inch) piece of fresh root ginger, peeled and very finely chopped
2 green chillies, very finely chopped
2 garlic cloves, very finely chopped
1 egg, beaten
1 tablespoon sesame seeds, toasted

To serve
sweet chilli dipping sauce
rice noodle salad with chopped peanuts, sliced onion, bean sprouts and chopped fresh coriander (optional)

Place the chicken in a large bowl with the lemon grass, kaffir lime leaves, ginger, chillies and garlic, which need to be so finely chopped as to almost make a paste. Add the beaten egg and sesame seeds. Mix well, using your hands.

Heat a griddle or frying pan. Divide the mixture into 16 and shape into small patties. Cook for 8 minutes on each side until cooked through.

Serve the chicken cakes with sweet chilli dipping sauce and a salad of rice noodles, chopped peanuts, sliced onion, bean sprouts and chopped coriander, if liked.

AWARENESS POINTS

- Try and find a local Asian supermarket to get the most aromatic kaffir lime leaves on offer. If you nibble on a dried leaf, can you detect a bitterness around the stalk?
- The lemon grass stalk should feel firm and heavy if it is fresh – it may have dried out if it is too light. As you chop the lemon grass notice the wood-like texture.
- Notice the crunch of the peanuts and beansprouts – how do the soft rice noodles offset this?

Baked fish with lemon grass

Calories per serving 284
(not including rice or vegetables)
Serves 4
Preparation time 10 minutes
Cooking time 20–25 minutes

1 kg (2 lb) whole fish (such as mackerel, sea bream or grey mullet), cleaned and scaled (if necessary), gutted and scored 3–4 times with a sharp knife

4 x 12 cm (5 inch) lemon grass stalks, cut diagonally into 2.5 cm (1 inch) lengths

2 carrots, cut into matchsticks

4 tablespoons light soy sauce

2 tablespoons lime juice

1 red chilli, finely chopped, plus extra slices to serve

To garnish
coriander leaves
a few wedges of lemon, to serve

AWARENESS POINTS

- Always source your fish ethically.
- Taste the light soy sauce mindfully. How is dark soy sauce different?
- Eat slowly, taking time to appreciate how the tender fish melts on your tongue.

Place the fish in a baking dish and sprinkle with the lemon grass, carrots, 1½ tablespoons of the light soy sauce and the lime juice.

Cover the baking dish with foil and bake in a preheated oven, 180°C (350°F), Gas Mark 4, for 20–25 minutes or until a skewer will slide easily into the flesh and come out clean. Place the fish on a warm serving plate and spoon over the sauce. Garnish with coriander leaves and chilli and serve with the lemon wedges.

Spoon the remaining light soy sauce into a small bowl with the chilli and serve separately. Serve with other dishes, with boiled rice or on its own as a light meal with stir-fried or steamed vegetables.

Smoked mustard chicken

Calories per serving 345
(not including broccoli)
Serves 4
Preparation time 10 minutes
Cooking time 20 minutes

1 tablespoon wholegrain mustard
1 tablespoon extra-virgin olive oil
4 skinned and boneless chicken breasts,
    about 175 g (6 oz) each
150 g (5 oz) uncooked rice
75 g (3 oz) Earl Grey tea leaves
salt and pepper

For the salsa verde
handful of flat leaf parsley
handful of mint leaves
handful of basil leaves
1 teaspoon capers
2 anchovies in oil
1 garlic clove, crushed
4 tablespoons olive oil
1 tablespoon red wine vinegar

AWARENESS POINTS

- Appreciate the process of
  smoking chicken from scratch.
  Celebrate that you have learnt
  a new skill.
- What is more sour tasting –
  the capers or the anchovies?
- Enjoy blending the aromatic
  ingredients of salsa verde,
  noting how the smell increases
  when the herbs are crushed.

Stir together the mustard and extra-vrigin olive oil in a
bowl and season with salt and pepper. Rub this mixture
all over the chicken breasts and set aside.

Prepare a wok for smoking by lining it with foil, then add
the rice and tea leaves, mixed together. Place a circular
rack in the wok and place the wok over a high heat with
the lid on. Heat until smoke starts to escape out of it.

Remove the lid and quickly sit the chicken on the rack.
Replace the lid and cook for 3 minutes, then reduce the
heat to medium and cook for a further 10 minutes.
Turn the heat off and let the chicken sit in the wok for
a further 5 minutes while you prepare the salsa verde.

Blend all the salsa verde ingredients in a mini food
processor or chop them up finely by hand. Tip into
a bowl and adjust the seasoning to taste. Serve the
chicken warm or at room temperature with the salsa
verde on the side and steamed vegetables such
as tenderstem broccoli, if liked.

Quick prosciutto & rocket pizza

Calories per serving 498

Serves 4

Preparation time 10 minutes

Cooking time 10 minutes

4 mini pizza bases

2 garlic cloves, halved

250 g (8 oz) reduced-fat mozzarella
  cheese, shredded

8 cherry tomatoes, quartered

150 g (5 oz) prosciutto, sliced

50 g (2 oz) rocket leaves, washed

balsamic vinegar, to taste

salt and pepper

Rub the top surfaces of the pizza bases with the cut faces of the garlic cloves. Transfer the bases to a baking sheet, top with mozzarella and tomatoes and bake in a preheated oven, 200°C (400°F), Gas Mark 6, for 10 minutes until the bread is golden.

Top the pizzas with slices of prosciutto and rocket leaves, season to taste with salt, pepper and balsamic vinegar and serve immediately.

AWARENESS POINTS

- Notice how the garlic juice feels on your fingertips.
- Consider how the smell of baking pizza makes you feel – excited, cosy, warm?
- Top your pizza decoratively, thinking about colours and shapes.

Roast pork with fennel

Calories per serving 451

Serves 4

Preparation time 10 minutes

Cooking time 30 minutes

625 g (1¼ lb) pork fillet

1 large rosemary sprig, broken into short lengths, plus extra sprigs to garnish

3 garlic cloves, sliced

4 tablespoons olive oil

1 large fennel bulb, trimmed and cut into wedges, central core removed

1 large red onion, cut into wedges

1 large red pepper, cored, deseeded and cut into chunks

150 ml (¼ pint) white wine

75 g (3 oz) mascarpone cheese (optional)

salt and pepper

AWARENESS POINTS

- Take the time to position the rosemary sprigs and garlic evenly – the more nooks and crannies you cover, the more fragrant the meat will be.
- Fennel is an acquired taste – note the sweet aniseed flavour. Are there other similar-tasting ingredients you like or dislike?
- Taste the pork meat, looking for specific parts where the rosemary and garlic have infused the flesh.

Pierce the pork with a sharp knife and insert the pieces of rosemary and garlic evenly all over the fillet. Heat half the oil in a roasting tin on the hob, add the pork and cook for 5 minutes or until browned all over.

Add the fennel, onion and red pepper to the roasting tin and drizzle the vegetables with the remaining oil. Season well with salt and pepper. Roast in a preheated oven, 230°C (450°F), Gas Mark 8, for 20 minutes or until the juices run clear when the pork is pierced in the centre with a knife.

Transfer the pork and vegetables to a serving plate and keep hot in the oven. Add the wine to the roasting tin and simmer on the hob until slightly reduced. Stir in the mascarpone, if using.

Cut the pork into slices and arrange on 4 serving plates with spoonfuls of the roasted vegetables and a spoonful or two of the sauce. Serve immediately, garnished with rosemary sprigs.

Beef fillet with red pepper crust

Calories per serving 302
   (not including wholegrain rice)

Serves 4

Preparation time 15 minutes

Cooking time about 30 minutes

1 red pepper, halved and deseeded

2 garlic cloves

8 dry black olives, pitted

1 tablespoon olive oil

2 teaspoons capers

8 shallots, peeled

50 ml (2 fl oz) balsamic vinegar

1 teaspoon light muscovado sugar

4 beef fillet steaks, about 150 g (5 oz)
   each

salt and pepper

AWARENESS POINTS

- Notice the changing texture of the pepper: from crunchy to soft to blended.

- Taste the rich, meaty beef and note what the sweet onions add to the experience.

- Really think about how hungry you are: can you serve a small spoonful of rice? Do you need rice at all?

Cook the red pepper under a preheated hot grill until the skin blackens. Remove and cover with damp kitchen paper until it is cool enough to handle, then peel the skin off and chop.

In a food processor, blend together the garlic, olives, 1 teaspoon of the oil, the capers and the chopped red pepper.

Put the shallots and the remaining oil in a small pan. Cover and cook over a low heat for 15 minutes, stirring frequently. Add the vinegar and sugar and cook uncovered for a further 5 minutes, stirring frequently.

Meanwhile, season the steaks and cook, 2 at a time, in a preheated heavy-based frying pan or griddle pan. Cook on one side for 2 minutes, then transfer to a baking sheet. Top each steak with some red pepper mix. Bake in a preheated oven, 200°C (400°F), Gas Mark 6, for 5 minutes or according to taste. Leave to rest in a warm place for 5 minutes before serving with the balsamic shallots and, if liked, steamed wholegrain rice and rocket leaves.

Haddock parcels & coconut rice

Calories per serving 340

Serves 4

Preparation time 15 minutes

Cooking time 20 minutes

4 haddock fillets, about
150 g (5 oz) each

4 tablespoons chopped fresh coriander

1 red chilli, chopped

1 shallot, finely sliced

1 lime, sliced, plus extra lime halves
to serve

2 lemon grass stalks, 1 roughly chopped
and 1 bashed

200 g (7 oz) Thai jasmine rice

400 ml (14 fl oz) water

2 fresh or dried kaffir lime leaves

50 ml (2 fl oz) reduced-fat coconut milk

AWARENESS POINTS

- Slice your ingredients delicately
  to suit the delicate flavours
  – the coriander and shallots
  should be as prominent as the
  strong chilli and lime.
- Arrange the parcels with care
  so that they will be attractive
  when opened – think of the
  process like wrapping
  a present.
- Savour the smells of warm,
  exotic lemon grass and
  coconut. How does the milk
  change the consistency of the
  rice? Does this wetter texture
  increase your appetite?

Cut 4 pieces of nonstick baking paper, each 30 cm
(12 inches) square. Put a haddock fillet in the centre
of each piece and arrange some of the coriander, chilli,
shallot, lime and chopped lemon grass stalk evenly over
each. Wrap them up into neat parcels.

Transfer the parcels to a baking sheet and cook
in a preheated oven, 180°C (350°F), Gas Mark 4,
for 20 minutes until the fish is cooked through.

Meanwhile, put the rice in a pan with the water, the
bashed lemon grass stalk and the lime leaves. Cover and
simmer for 12 minutes. When the rice is cooked and the
water absorbed, stir in the coconut milk. Serve with the
haddock parcels, with some extra lime halves.

Lemon grass chicken

Calories per serving 476

Serves 4

Preparation time 15 minutes

Cooking time 1¾–2¼ hours

1 tablespoon sunflower oil

12 large chicken drumsticks (remove skin before eating)

1 onion, finely chopped

4 garlic cloves, crushed

6 tablespoons very finely chopped lemon grass and 1 lemon grass stalk, halved lengthways

1 red chilli, finely sliced or chopped

2 tablespoons medium curry paste

1 tablespoon grated palm sugar

250 ml (8 fl oz) chicken stock

salt and pepper

AWARENESS POINTS

- See if you can buy organic chicken.
- Enjoy the slow cooking process and take this time to pursue a hobby or meditate.
- Mark the way the tender chicken falls from the bone and 'melts' as you eat it.

Heat the oil in a large, heavy-based casserole dish and brown the drumsticks evenly for 5–6 minutes. Remove with a slotted spoon and set aside.

Add the onion and stir-fry over a low heat for 10 minutes. Add the garlic, chopped lemon grass, chilli and curry paste and stir-fry for 1–2 minutes.

Return the chicken to the dish with the palm sugar and stock. Bring to the boil, season and cover tightly. Cook in a preheated oven, 140°C (275°F), Gas Mark 1, for 1½–2 hours or until tender and cooked through. Remove from the oven and serve immediately.

Okra & coconut stew

Calories per serving 421

Serves 4

Preparation time 15 minutes

Cooking time 40 minutes

375 g (12 oz) okra

4 tablespoons vegetable oil

2 onions, chopped

2 green peppers, cored, deseeded
   and cut into chunks

3 celery sticks, thinly sliced

3 garlic cloves, crushed

4 teaspoons Cajun spice blend

½ teaspoon ground turmeric

300 ml (½ pint) vegetable stock

400 ml (14 fl oz) can coconut milk

200 g (7 oz) frozen sweetcorn

juice of 1 lime

4 tablespoons chopped fresh coriander

salt and pepper

Trim the stalk ends from the okra and cut the pods into 1.5 cm (¾ inch) lengths.

Heat 2 tablespoons of the oil in a large deep-sided frying pan or shallow flameproof casserole and fry the okra for 5 minutes. Lift out with a slotted spoon on to a plate.

Add the remaining oil to the pan and very gently fry the onions, peppers and celery for 10 minutes until softened but not browned, stirring frequently. Add the garlic, spice blend and turmeric and cook for 1 minute.

Pour in the stock and coconut milk and bring to the boil. Reduce the heat, cover and cook gently for 10 minutes. Return the okra to the pan with the sweetcorn, lime juice and coriander and cook for a further 10 minutes. Season to taste with salt and pepper and serve.

AWARENESS POINTS

- Note the intricacy of the okra – the tessellated pattern and ridged shape.
- Mark the deep yellow of the turmeric. Be careful of it staining your hands and white crockery.
- Enjoy delving into the stew with its many textures and layers.

Aubergine parcels with pine nuts

Calories per serving 436

Serves 2

Preparation time 30 minutes, plus
chilling

Cooking time 12–15 minutes

1 tablespoon pine nuts

1 long, large aubergine

125 g (4 oz) mozzarella cheese

1 large or 2 small plum tomatoes

8 large basil leaves, plus extra, torn,
to garnish

1 tablespoon olive oil

salt and pepper

Tomato dressing

2 tablespoons olive oil

1 teaspoon balsamic vinegar

1 teaspoon sun-dried
tomato paste

1 teaspoon lemon juice

AWARENESS POINTS

- Explore the rubbery texture of
  the mozzarella. Do you know
  how it is made?
- Pay attention to the tightness
  of the parcels and the layers
  inside – neat and even will get
  best results.
- You may find that your
  technique gets better as you go
  along so don't be critical.

Make the dressing. Whisk together the oil, vinegar, tomato paste and lemon juice in a small bowl. Set aside.

Dry-fry the pine nuts in a hot pan until golden brown. Remove from the pan and set aside.

Cut the stalk off the aubergine and cut it lengthways to give 8 slices (disregarding the ends). Cook the slices in a saucepan of boiling salted water for 2 minutes. Drain and dry on kitchen paper. Cut the mozzarella into 4 slices and the tomato into 8 slices (disregarding the outer edges).

Put 2 aubergine slices in an ovenproof dish, forming an X-shape. Put a slice of tomato on top, season with salt and pepper, add a basil leaf, a slice of mozzarella, another basil leaf, then more salt and pepper, and finally another slice of tomato. Fold the edges of the aubergine around the filling to make a parcel. Repeat with the other ingredients to make 4 parcels in total. Cover and chill in the refrigerator for 20 minutes.

Brush the aubergine parcels with the oil. Put the dish under a preheated hot grill and cook for about 5 minutes on each side until golden-brown. Serve 2 parcels per person, drizzled with the dressing, and scattered with the pine nuts and torn basil leaves.

Chicken with orange & mint

Calories per serving 355
   (not including couscous)

Serves 4

Preparation time 5 minutes

Cooking time 15–20 minutes

4 boneless, skinless chicken breasts,
   about 200 g (7 oz) each

3 tablespoons olive oil

150 ml (¼ pint) freshly squeezed
   orange juice

1 small orange, sliced

2 tablespoons chopped mint

1 tablespoon butter

salt and pepper

AWARENESS POINTS

- Buy organic chicken and know
  your food source.
- Smell the fresh mint and the
  citrus tang of orange.
- Take slow bites and consider
  the mix of flavours – can you
  taste each one?

Season the chicken breasts to taste with salt and pepper.
Heat the oil in a large nonstick frying pan, add the
chicken breasts and cook over a medium heat for 4–5
minutes or until golden all over, turning once.

Pour in the orange juice, add the orange slices and bring
to a gentle simmer. Cover tightly, reduce the heat to low
and cook gently for 8–10 minutes or until the chicken
is cooked through. Add the chopped mint and butter
and stir to mix well. Cook over a high heat, stirring, for
2 minutes. Serve with couscous, if liked.

Guided practice

The soup in the first recipe here combines chunks of delicious squash with protein-rich beans and bright green, vitamin-rich kale. Its liquid stock and its vegetable content mean that the body will be refreshed by fluids, as well as food nutrients.

1 Vegetables can be the key ingredients of light meals, suitable for summertime or lunches on the go, but they can also be combined to create comforting, satisfying dishes. Sweet potatoes, butternut squash and root vegetables, such as swede or carrots, can be roasted or used in hearty stews and soups. Green vegetables provide a bitter and refreshing flavour contrast, and are packed full of iron and vitamin C, essential for a healthy body. Beans are cheap to buy, and provide a great, low-fat way of taking in protein and fibre, perfect for achieving and keeping the feeling of a full stomach, and healthy digestion.

2 Appreciate the changing aromas as the onion, garlic and spices fry together when you begin cooking. Notice the subtle changes as you add ingredients. As the combined ingredients cook, notice that their juices blend with the stock to swell the soup, even as some liquid bubbles away in the cooking process.

3 Taste the soup carefully, testing the seasoning as you go. Check the texture of the vegetables – perhaps you prefer them with a bit of crunch. Let it cool gently before you begin to eat it. Use a wide, flat spoon, and sip the liquid slowly, taking care to chew the vegetables and paying attention to way the soup's warmth affects how your body feels.

Squash, kale & mixed bean soup

Calories per serving 182
(not including garlic bread)
Serves 6
Preparation time 15 minutes
Cooking time 45 minutes

1 tablespoon olive oil
1 onion, finely chopped
2 garlic cloves, finely chopped
1 teaspoon smoked paprika
500 g (1 lb) butternut squash, halved,
    deseeded, peeled and diced
2 small carrots, peeled
and diced
500 g (1 lb) tomatoes, skinned (optional)
    and roughly chopped
400 g (13 oz) can mixed beans,
    rinsed and drained
900 ml (1½ pints) hot vegetable stock
150 ml (¼ pint) half-fat crème fraîche
100 g (3½ oz) kale, torn
    into bite-sized pieces
salt and pepper

Heat the oil in a saucepan over a medium-low heat, add the onion and fry gently for 5 minutes. Stir in the garlic and smoked paprika and cook briefly, then add the squash, carrots, tomatoes and mixed beans.

Pour in the stock, season with salt and pepper and bring to the boil, stirring frequently. Reduce the heat, cover and simmer for 25 minutes or until the vegetables are cooked and tender.

Stir in the crème fraîche, then add the kale, pressing it just beneath the surface of the stock. Cover and cook for 5 minutes or until the kale has just wilted. Ladle into bowls and serve with warm garlic bread, if liked.

Salmon curry with tomato salad

Calories per serving 477
Serves 2
Preparation time 10 minutes
Cooking time 20–25 minutes

1 teaspoon vegetable oil
1 small onion, sliced
1 garlic clove, chopped
1 teaspoon tandoori spice mix
1 cinnamon stick
150 g (5 oz) cherry tomatoes, halved
4 tablespoons reduced-fat crème
    fraîche
grated rind and juice of ½ lime
175 g (6 oz) skinless salmon fillet, cut
    into chunks
1 tablespoon chopped mint
1 tablespoon chopped fresh coriander

Tomato & onion salad

150 g (5 oz) vine-ripened tomatoes,
    thinly sliced
1 small red onion, finely sliced
handful of fresh coriander, chopped
1 teaspoon lemon juice

Heat the oil in a small frying pan, add the onion and garlic and fry for 2–3 minutes until softened. Stir in the spice mix and cinnamon stick and fry for 1 further minute. Add the tomatoes, crème fraîche, lime rind and juice and heat for 1 minute.

Put the salmon in an ovenproof dish. Spoon over the sauce, cover the dish tightly with foil and cook in a preheated oven, 200°C (400°F), Gas Mark 6, for 15–20 minutes or until the salmon is just cooked through.

Meanwhile, make the salad. Toss together the tomatoes, onion and coriander. and dress with lemon juice. Serve the salmon with the tomato and onion salad.

AWARENESS POINTS

- Make sure your salmon is from a sustainable source. Adapt the recipe with a sustainable fish if not.
- Choose the sweetest, reddest tomatoes for the fullest flavour.
- Taste the sauce before and after the crème fraîche and notice the changes.

Lentil moussaka

Calories per serving 304

Serves 4

Preparation time 10 minutes

Cooking time 45–50 minutes,
  plus standing

125 g (4 oz) dried brown or green lentils,
  rinsed and drained
400 g (13 oz) can chopped tomatoes
2 garlic cloves, crushed
½ teaspoon dried oregano
pinch of ground nutmeg
150 ml (¼ pint) vegetable stock,
  plus extra if needed
2–3 tablespoons vegetable oil
250 g (8 oz) aubergine, sliced
1 onion, finely chopped

Cheese topping

1 egg
150 g (5 oz) soft cheese
pinch of ground nutmeg
salt and pepper

Put the lentils in a saucepan with the tomatoes, garlic, oregano and nutmeg. Pour in the stock. Bring to the boil, then reduce the heat and simmer for 20 minutes until the lentils are tender but not mushy, topping up with extra stock as needed.

Meanwhile, heat the oil in a frying pan and lightly fry the aubergine and onion until the onion is soft and the aubergine is golden on both sides.

Layer the aubergine mixture and lentil mixture alternately in an ovenproof dish.

Make the topping. In a bowl, beat together the egg, cheese and nutmeg with a good dash of salt and pepper. Pour over the moussaka and cook in a preheated oven, 200°C (400°F), Gas Mark 6, for 20–25 minutes. Remove from the oven and leave to stand for 5 minutes before serving with salad leaves.

AWARENESS POINTS

- Appreciate nutmeg as a powerful ingredient – the Chinese used it for inflammation, the Roman civilizations used it for stress relief and it has been known to ease indigestion.
- Enjoy the contrasting layers in the slices of moussaka – does it feel like a richer, more filling meal?
- Serve small portions, and eat slowly: lentils and eggs are filling foods.

Chicken wrapped in parma ham

Calories per serving 431

Serves 4

Preparation time 10 minutes

Cooking time about 10 minutes

4 boneless, skinless chicken breasts, about 150 g (5 oz) each

4 slices of Parma ham

4 sage leaves

plain flour, for dusting

25 g (1 oz) butter

2 tablespoons olive oil

4 sprigs cherry tomatoes on the vine

150 ml (¼ pint) dry white wine

salt and pepper

AWARENESS POINTS

- Notice the smell and texture of sage leaves – how downy are they?
- How do the sweet cherry tomatoes contrast the salty ham?
- This is a great example of using awareness to ensure your chicken is safe and fully-cooked – make sure the juices run clear.

Lay each chicken breast between 2 sheets of clingfilm and flatten with a rolling pin or meat mallet until wafer thin. Season with salt and pepper.

Lay a slice of Parma ham on each chicken breast, followed by a sage leaf. Secure the sage and ham in position with a cocktail stick, then lightly dust both sides of the chicken with flour. Season again with salt and pepper.

Heat the butter and oil in a large frying pan over a high heat, add the chicken and cook for 4–5 minutes on each side or until the juices run clear when pierced with a knife. Add the tomatoes and wine to the pan and bubble until the wine has thickened and reduced by about half. Serve immediately, accompanied by a green salad.

Chilli pork with pineapple rice

Calories per serving 440

Serves 4

Preparation time 20 minutes,
 plus marinating

Cooking time 15 minutes

2 tablespoons sunflower oil

2 tablespoons lime juice

2 garlic cloves, crushed

1 red chilli, deseeded and finely
 chopped

300 g (10 oz) pork fillet, cubed

200 g (7 oz) Thai fragrant rice

6 spring onions, finely sliced

200 g (7 oz) pineapple, peeled and diced

½ red onion, cut into wedges

1 lime, cut into wedges

salt and pepper

ready-made sweet chilli sauce, to serve

Presoak 8 wooden skewers in warm water. Mix together the oil, lime juice, garlic, chilli and salt and pepper in a bowl, add the pork and stir to coat. Cover and leave to marinate in the refridgerator for at least 1 hour.

Cook the rice in lightly salted boiling water for 12–15 minutes or according to the instructions on the packet. Drain and stir through the spring onions and pineapple.

Meanwhile, thread the pork on to the skewers, alternating it with onion and lime wedges, and cook under a preheated hot grill for about 10 minutes, turning frequently and basting with the remaining marinade, until the pork is cooked through.

Put the skewers and rice on a plate with the sweet chilli sauce and serve immediately.

AWARENESS POINTS

- Load your skewers with an eye to the visual – make a pattern.
- Taste the dish mindfully, noting sweet and sour in turn.
- Serve the sauce in a favourite bowl or saucer.

Malaysian rendang lamb

Calories per serving 455

Serves 6

Preparation time 15 minutes,
plus standing

Cooking time 2¾ hours

2 tablespoons sunflower oil

800 g (1 lb 10 oz) leg of lamb, butterflied

2 onions, finely chopped

1 tablespoon ground coriander

1 teaspoon ground turmeric

6 garlic cloves, crushed

6 tablespoons very finely chopped
lemon grass

4–6 bird's eye chillies, chopped

4 tablespoons finely chopped fresh
coriander root and stem

400 ml (14 fl oz) can reduced-fat
coconut milk

salt and pepper

Heat the oil in a deep, heavy-based casserole dish and brown the lamb on both sides for about 5–6 minutes.

Place the remaining ingredients in a food processor and blend until smooth. Season well.

Pour this mixture over the lamb and bring to the boil. Cover tightly and place in a preheated oven at 150°C (300°F), Gas Mark 2 for 2½ hours, turning occasionally, until the lamb is meltingly tender and most of the liquid has evaporated.

Remove from the oven and leave to stand for about 10–12 minutes before serving, cut into thick slices.

AWARENESS POINTS

- This can be a very impressive dish to serve to friends. Think about who you would like to treat.
- Allow the recommended full cooking and standing time, build up to a sense of occasion, let your appetite reach a healthy level and your mind unwind from any emotional stress.
- Notice the melting, tender texture of each mouthful of lamb.

Seafood & vegetable stir-fry

Calories per serving 220
  (not including the rice)

Serves 4

Preparation time 20 minutes

Cooking time 7–10 minutes

250 g (8 oz) live mussels

250 g (8 oz) water chestnuts, peeled
  and thickly sliced

1 tablespoon caster sugar

½ teaspoon black pepper

2 tablespoons vegetable oil

1 sweet white onion, sliced

125 g (4 oz) raw peeled tiger prawns

4 spring onions, diagonally sliced

½ teaspoon crushed chilli flakes, plus
  extra to garnish

125 g (4 oz) sugar snap peas, trimmed
  and diagonally halved

125 g (4 oz) bean sprouts

3 tablespoons light soy sauce

2 tablespoons yellow bean sauce

2 tablespoons Chinese rice wine
  or dry sherry

chervil sprigs, to garnish

AWARENESS POINTS

- Vary your vegetables according
  to season and source locally.
- Inhale and appreciate the hot,
  spicy steam from your wok.
- Enjoy the contrast of the
  softly chewy mussels and the
  crunchy veg.

Scrub the mussels thoroughly under cold running water.
Pull off the hairy 'beards' and rinse again. Gently tap any
open mussels and discard any that do not close.

Sprinkle the water chestnuts with the sugar and pepper
and set aside.

Heat the oil in a wok over a high heat until the oil starts
to shimmer. Add the onion and mussels and stir-fry
quickly for 1 minute. Put a lid on the wok and cook for
3–4 minutes or until the mussels have opened. Discard
any mussels that remain closed.

Add the water chestnuts, prawns, spring onions, chilli
flakes, sugar snaps and bean sprouts to the wok and stir-
fry for 1–2 minutes or until the prawns have turned pink
and are cooked through.

Mix together the soy sauce, yellow bean sauce and rice
wine or sherry and pour over the ingredients in the wok.
Stir-fry for a further 1–2 minutes until hot. Garnish with
crushed chilli flakes and chervil sprigs. Serve with rice.

Mushroom stroganoff

Calories per serving 239
Serves 4
Preparation time 10 minutes
Cooking time 10 minutes

1 tablespoon butter
2 tablespoons olive oil
1 onion, thinly sliced
4 garlic cloves, finely chopped
500 g (1 lb) chestnut mushrooms, sliced
2 tablespoons wholegrain mustard
250 ml (8 fl oz) half-fat
   crème fraîche
salt and pepper
3 tablespoons chopped parsley,
   to garnish

Heat the butter and oil in a large frying pan,
add the onion and garlic and cook until soft and
starting to brown.

Add the mushrooms to the pan and cook until soft
and starting to brown. Stir in the mustard and crème
fraîche and just heat through. Season to taste with
salt and pepper, then serve immediately, garnished
with the chopped parsley.

AWARENESS POINTS

- Taste the wholegrain mustard
  and mark the sweetness and
  heat. How does it compare to
  English or American mustard?
- Notice the satisfying, meaty
  texture of the mushrooms.
- This recipe is incredibly simple
  to make – how will you spend
  the extra time?

Burmese chicken noodle curry

Calories per serving 403

Serves 6

Preparation time 20 minutes

Cooking time about 1 hour

1 kg (2 lb) boneless, skinless chicken
thighs, cut into bite-sized pieces

2 onions, chopped

5 garlic cloves, chopped

1 teaspoon peeled and finely grated
fresh root ginger

2 tablespoons sunflower oil

½ teaspoon Burmese shrimp paste
(belacan)

400 ml (14 fl oz) can coconut milk

1 tablespoon medium curry powder

300 g (10½ oz) dried rice vermicelli

salt and pepper

To garnish

chopped fresh coriander

finely chopped red onion

fried garlic slivers

sliced fresh red chillies

lime wedges

Season the chicken pieces and set aside. Process the onion, garlic and ginger in a food processor until smooth. If necessary, add a little water to assist in blending the mixture. Heat the oil in a large pan. Add the onion mixture and shrimp paste and cook, stirring, over a high heat for about 5 minutes.

Add the chicken and cook over a medium heat, turning it until it browns.

Pour in the coconut milk and add the curry powder. Bring to the boil, reduce the heat, cover and simmer, covered, for about 30 minutes, stirring occasionally. Uncover the pan and cook for a further 15 minutes or until the chicken is tender and cooked through.

Meanwhile, place the noodles in a bowl, cover with boiling water and set aside for 10 minutes. Drain the noodles and divide them between 4 large warmed serving bowls. Ladle over the curry, and garnish with chopped coriander, chopped red onion, fried garlic slivers, sliced red chillies and lime wedges.

AWARENESS POINTS

- Buy free–range organic chicken thighs if you can.
- Shrimp paste can be extremely pungent – note how the smell diffuses after cooking.
- Be slow and meticulous in finely slicing your garnishes.

Mindful treats

Guilt food – how to deal with cravings

This book is based on the idea that behind every weight problem is a human being. Most of us have dieted or have seen friends losing and gaining weight. Most diets don't work because they deal with food intake only, not with the human being who consumes it. We gain weight because we eat when we are not hungry; we become too thin when we deprive ourselves of food when we do need it. In both cases, the mind overrides simple body symptoms and tries to solve unpleasant moods and feelings by eating, or not eating.

We all look for quick solutions to our inner dissatisfactions by seeking satisfying experiences through food. Unfortunately, this doesn't work. We can get satisfaction through food when we are hungry, but we can't feed the longings of our mind with food. We have to learn to differentiate between the needs of our body and the needs and desires of our mind and soul.

In this exercise you will gain more insight into the triggers that make you eat even when you are not hungry. As you become more aware of the moments before you fall into your unhelpful eating pattern, you will find it easier to change it. You will slowly unlock the origin of dissatisfaction and hurt that is keeping these thinking and behaviour patterns in place. Having done this, you can start to find other ways – developing new neuro pathways – of dealing with unhappiness and pain.

A WEEK WITHOUT

Try giving up any one of the following for a week, and explore the experience:

sugar
snacks
your favourite caffeine
dairy food
white flour
alcohol
meat
pre-packed food
complaining
internet
mobile phone
car

The flesh is willing... what are your food triggers?

The point of this exercise is to become more aware of what happens just prior to indulging in food or drink, to help you spot the most irresistible triggers.

• Begin by putting your hand on your heart or solar plexus and visualizing being cradled by overflowing compassion. You may want to see somebody who symbolizes kindness for you.

• Review how your overeating or undereating has harmed you and others, and think about how you would like to change this destructive pattern.

• Help your mind to slow down and relax by bringing awareness to your breathing for a little while.

• Fill your mind with care and compassion, and the will to transform your behaviour. Allow yourself to be nurtured by this energy.

• Then shift your memory to the last time you overindulged in food. Recall the moment it started, and then go back an instant to when you were just about to start engaging in your addictive behaviour. Contemplate what was occurring during that moment. Find out what this starting point feels like.

• Try to bring vivid awareness to your surroundings at that time. Imagine this is all happening right now. Can you see yourself and where you are? Are there any people nearby or are you alone? What odours are present? What tastes do you notice in your mouth and what sounds can you hear? Is your body sensitive or numb? Are you physically and mentally comfortable or uncomfortable?

Any of these factors could be an external trigger. View it with composure and slight detachment, as you would look at a photograph or as if you were a CCTV camera just filming but not reacting to what is recorded.

• Carry on deepening your awareness of what was occurring at that time. Were you in any pain? Did you feel stressed? Were you trying to calm down? Had you just been involved in an argument? Did you feel lonesome? Had someone upset you or had you frustrated yourself? Were you trying to impress anyone? Did life feel disappointing? Was it difficult to cope?

Any of these could have been internal triggers. View them peacefully and with kindness. Remain aware of that moment as long as you possibly can. Pinpoint those factors that set you off. Accept that this is your current reality, and is the way in which you cope with difficulties for now.

Guided practice

Everything in moderation. There are many ways to celebrate food and the act of having something to eat as a reward can be interpreted with a more mindful approach. For example, rather than assuming an unhealthy chocolate cake will boost your mood or transform your stressful day, stop and think about what you actually need. Be true to your body's signals and sensations. It may be that you need to drink more water or boost low blood sugar. In this book, there is no suggestion of giving up your favourite foods and indulgences; simply widen your perception when it comes to treating yourself with food. Is there a healthier alternative? Can you give up caffeine for a week and explore the experience? And when you do treat yourself with food, are you getting the most out of it – savouring every taste sensation rather than eating on autopilot?

1 The first recipe here, for chocolate Florentines, is a perfect example of eating something very decadent and delicious in moderation. One Florentine is crammed with textures and flavours to enjoy – flaked almonds, candied peel, rich dark chocolate. One tiny Florentine can contain a wealth of treats. The trick, of course, is to be mindful and not eat the whole lot!

2 When you add the dried ingredients, one by one, into the melted sugar and butter mixture, notice how different and wonderful they are – a cascade of roughly chopped glacé cherries, tumbling hazelnuts, small crystals of candied peel. There are hundreds of combinations of dried fruit and nuts to try.

3 As you spoon the mixture carefully on to the baking sheets, listen to the crackling of paper and notice the stickiness.

4 Notice the texture of the thin layer of precious, rich, dark chocolate as you spread it on the Florentines.

5 Finally, when you come to eat your compact treat, notice the different sweet tastes and textures with every nibble – the sharpness of the candied peel, the smooth, sweet but bitter chocolate and the crunchy almond flakes. See if you can make a list of 10-20 different sensations. Read it back to yourself and see how one treat can be enhanced with a complex, mindful approach.

Florentines

Calories per serving 126
Makes 26
Preparation time 20 minutes, plus cooling
Cooking time 20–25 minutes

100 g (3½ oz) butter
100 g (3½ oz) caster sugar
75 g (3 oz) multicoloured glacé cherries,
   roughly chopped
75 g (3 oz) flaked almonds
50 g (2 oz) whole candied peel, finely chopped
50 g (2 oz) hazelnuts, roughly chopped
2 tablespoons plain flour
150 g (5 oz) plain dark chocolate,
   broken into pieces

Put the butter and sugar in a saucepan and heat gently until the butter has melted and the sugar dissolved. Remove the pan from the heat and stir in all the remaining ingredients except the chocolate.

Spoon tablespoons of the mixture, well spaced apart, on to 3 baking sheets lined with nonstick baking paper. Flatten the mounds slightly. Cook 1 baking sheet at a time in the centre of a preheated oven, 180°C (350°F), Gas Mark 4, for 5–7 minutes until the nuts are golden.

After removing each baking sheet from the oven, neaten and shape the cooked biscuits by placing a slightly larger plain round biscuit cutter over the top and rotating to smooth and tidy up the edges. Leave to cool.

Melt the chocolate in a heatproof bowl set over a saucepan of gently simmering water. Peel the biscuits off the lining paper and arrange upside down on a wire rack. Spoon the melted chocolate over the flat underside of the biscuits and spread the surfaces level. Leave to cool and harden.

Black forest brownies

Calories per serving 317
(not including chocolate sauce)

Cuts into 12

Preparation time 25 minutes,
plus cooling

Cooking time 25–30 minutes

125 g (4 oz) slightly salted butter, plus
extra for greasing

150 g (5 oz) plain dark chocolate,
chopped

2 eggs

175 g (6 oz) dark muscovado sugar

1 teaspoon vanilla extract

50 g (2 oz) self-raising flour

200 g (7 oz) black or red cherries, pitted
and halved, plus extra to serve

To serve

150 ml (¼ pint) double cream

chocolate shavings

AWARENESS POINTS

- Spoil yourself in true childhood
  fashion – after you have
  transferred the melted
  chocolate to the mixing bowl,
  lick the spoon a couple of
  times before you wash it.

- Compare the consistency of
  the melted chocolate, foamy
  egg mixture and the coarse
  combined mixture.

- Try and eat just one small
  square at a time – enjoy this a
  bite-sized, balanced treat.

Grease an 18 cm (7 inch) square cake tinn of shallow
baking tin and line it with nonstick baking paper.

Melt 50 g (2 oz) of the chocolate and the butter in a
heatproof bowl set over a saucepan of gently simmering
water (don't let the base of the bowl touch the water).
Beat the eggs, sugar and vanilla extract in a separate
bowl until light and foamy. Stir in the melted chocolate
mixture. Tip in the flour, cherries and remaining
chocolate and mix together until just combined.

Spoon the mixture into the prepared tin and level the
surface. Bake in a preheated oven, 180°C (350°F), Gas
Mark 4, for 20–25 minutes or until just firm to the touch.
Leave to cool in the tin, then transfer to a board and peel
off the lining paper.

Whip the cream in a bowl until peaking, then spread
over the cake. Sprinkle with chocolate shavings and cut
into small squares. Serve with extra cherries and rich
chocolate sauce, if liked.

Mango & passion fruit brûlée

Calories per serving 202

Serves 4

Preparation time 10 minutes, plus chilling

Cooking time 1–2 minutes

1 small mango, peeled, stoned and thinly sliced

2 passion fruit, flesh scooped out

300 g (10 oz) low-fat natural yogurt

200 g (7 oz) half-fat crème fraîche

1 tablespoon icing sugar

few drops of vanilla extract

2 tablespoons demerara sugar

Arrange the mango slices in 4 ramekins.

Stir together the passion fruit flesh, yogurt, crème fraîche, icing sugar and vanilla extract in a bowl, then spoon the mixture over the mango. Tap each ramekin to level the surface.

Sprinkle over the demerara sugar and cook the brûlées under a preheated hot grill for 1–2 minutes until the sugar has melted. Chill for about 30 minutes, then serve.

For plum & peach brûlée, replace the mango with 2 sliced peaches. Continue as above, replacing the passion fruit with 4 firm but ripe chopped plums. Before grilling, top each ramekin with a piece of chopped crystallized ginger.

AWARENESS POINTS

- Notice the crack of the surface as you break into it.
- How does the sharp brittle texture feel on your tongue?
- Where in your mouth can you taste the passion fruit and vanilla?

Tuile baskets & strawberry cream

Calories per serving 404
Serves 6
Preparation time 40 minutes
Cooking time 15–18 minutes

2 egg whites
100 g (3½ oz) caster sugar
50 g (2 oz) unsalted butter, melted
few drops of vanilla extract
50 g (2 oz) plain flour

Strawberry cream
250 ml (8 fl oz) double cream
4 tablespoons icing sugar, plus extra
   for dusting
2 tablespoons chopped mint,
   plus extra leaves to decorate
250 g (8 oz) strawberries, hulled and
   halved or sliced, depending on size

AWARENESS POINTS

- Lay out the ingredients and
  savour the smell of the vanilla,
  mint and strawberries in turn.
  Which affects your appetite
  the most?
- Making the pleats and shaping
  the tuiles is intricate work so
  allow yourself extra time – let
  it be it a calm activity.
- How does the mint contrast the
  sweetness of the sugar?

Put the egg whites in a bowl and break up with a fork. Stir in the caster sugar, then the butter and vanilla extract. Sift in the flour and mix until smooth.

Drop 1 heaped tablespoon of the mixture on to a baking sheet lined with nonstick baking paper. Drop a second spoonful well apart from the first, then spread each into a thin circle about 13 cm (5 inches) in diameter. Bake in a preheated oven, 190°C (375°F), Gas Mark 5, for 5–6 minutes until just beginning to brown around the edges.

Add 2 more spoonfuls to a second paper-lined baking sheet and spread thinly. Remove the baked tuiles from the oven and put the second tray in. Leave the cooked tuiles to firm up for 5–10 seconds, then carefully lift them off the paper one at a time and drape each over an orange. Pinch the edges into pleats and leave to harden for 2–3 minutes, then carefully ease off. Repeat until 6 tuiles have been made.

Whip the cream lightly, then fold in the mint, the strawberries and nearly all of the icing the sugar, reserving 6 strawberry halves for decoration. Spoon into the tuiles, then top with the mint leaves and the strawberry halves. Sift with the remaining icing sugar.

Grilled fruits with palm sugar

Calories per serving 176
  (not including the ice cream)
Serves 4
Preparation time 10 minutes
Cooking time 6–16 minutes

25 g (1 oz) palm sugar
grated rind and juice of 1 lime
2 tablespoons water
½ teaspoon cracked black peppercorns
500 g (1 lb) mixed prepared fruits,
    such as pineapple or peach slices or
    mango wedges

To serve
cinnamon or vanilla ice cream
lime slices

Put the sugar, lime rind and juice, measurement water and peppercorns in a small saucepan and heat over a low heat until the sugar has dissolved. Plunge the base of the pan into iced water to cool.

Brush the cooled syrup over the prepared fruits and cook under a preheated hot grill for 6–8 minutes on each side, or over a preheated hot gas barbecue or the hot coals of a charcoal barbecue, for 3–4 minutes on each side until charred and tender.

Serve with scoops of cinnamon or vanilla ice cream and lime slices.

For grilled fruit kebabs, cut the prepared fruits into large chunks, thread on to wooden skewers, presoaked in cold water for 30 minutes, and brush with the cooled syrup before cooking as in the recipe above.

AWARENESS POINTS

- Try a drop of lime juice – does your face react to the sharp taste? Do the same with a piece of peppercorn and compare your reaction? Which do you prefer and why?
- How many shades of orange and yellow can you find in the different prepared fruits? Do these colours brighten your mood?
- If you use a barbecue, does the smell of the coals evoke any memories? What about the smell of cinnamon or vanilla?

Pomegranate & ginger slice

Calories per serving 121

Cuts into 20

Preparation time 25 minutes

Cooking time 50 minutes

200 g (7 oz) plain flour

1 teaspoon bicarbonate of soda

100 ml (3½ fl oz) milk

1 egg

100 g (3½ oz) dark muscovado sugar

125 g (4 oz) black treacle

75 g (3 oz) unsalted butter, plus extra
for greasing

3 pieces of stem ginger in syrup,
chopped

Topping

300 ml (½ pint) pomegranate juice

2 tablespoons clear honey

1 pomegranate

AWARENESS POINTS

- Note how the treacle changes the consistency of the mixture and then changes again as it dissolves.
- Be mindful of your storecupboard ingredients. Jarred ginger can be reused to spice up juices and smoothies or make a batch of gingerbread.
- Appreciate the pop of bold colour that the pomegranate adds to the dark brown bake.

Sift the flour and bicarbonate of soda into a bowl. Beat together the milk and egg in a jug. Put the sugar, treacle and butter in a saucepan and heat gently until the butter melts and the sugar dissolves. Remove from the heat and add to the milk mixture with the chopped ginger. Add to the dry ingredients and stir together using a large metal spoon until well combined.

Spoon the mixture into 2 greased and lined 1 kg (2 lb) loaf tins and level the surface. Bake in a preheated oven, 160°C (325°F), Gas Mark 3, for 30 minutes or until just firm to the touch and a skewer inserted into the centre comes out clean. Leave to cool in the tins, then loosen at the ends and transfer to a wire rack. Peel off the lining paper.

Make the topping. Pour the pomegranate juice into a saucepan and bring to the boil, then boil for about 15 minutes until thick and syrupy and reduced to about 3 tablespoons. Stir in the honey. Halve the pomegranate and push the halves inside out to release the fleshy seeds, discarding any white membrane. Scatter the seeds over the top of the cakes. Drizzle with the syrup and cut into 20 small squares to serve.

Chocolate, courgette & nut cake

Calories per serving 266

Serves 12

Preparation time 10–15 minutes,
   plus cooling

Cooking time 40 minutes

250 g (8 oz) courgettes, coarsely grated

2 eggs

100 ml (3 ½ fl oz) vegetable oil,
   plus extra for greasing

grated rind and juice of
1 orange

125 g (4 oz) caster sugar

225 g (7 ½ oz) self-raising flour

2 tablespoons cocoa powder

½ teaspoon bicarbonate of soda

½ teaspoon baking powder

50 g (2 oz) ready-to-eat dried apricots,
   chopped

Topping

200 g (7 oz) cream cheese

2 tablespoons chocolate hazelnut
   spread

1 tablespoon hazelnuts, toasted
   and chopped

Place the courgettes in a sieve and squeeze out any excess liquid.

Beat together the eggs, oil, orange rind and juice and sugar in a large bowl. Sift in the flour, cocoa powder, bicarbonate of soda and baking powder and beat to combine.

Fold in the courgettes and apricots, then spoon the mixture into a greased and lined 20 cm (8 inch) deep loose-based cake tin.

Bake in a preheated oven, 180°C (350°F), Gas Mark 4, for 40 minutes until risen and firm to the touch. Turn out on to a wire rack to cool.

Beat together the cream cheese and chocolate hazelnut spread and spread over the top of the cake. Sprinkle over the hazelnuts. Cut into 12 to serve.

AWARENESS POINTS

- Compare the bright green colour of the courgettes to the rich orange colour of the fruit and eggs. What do you usually associate with the colour green? Are you apprehensive about using courgettes in a cake?
- Taste the raw courgette and note its characteristics – can you spot the same taste once the cake is cooked or is it hidden?
- What is sweeter – the cake base or the cream cheese, hazelnut topping?

White chocolate mousse

Calories per serving 192

Serves 6–8

Preparation time 10 minutes,
   plus chilling

200 g (7 oz) white chocolate, chopped

4 tablespoons milk

12 cardamom pods

200 g (7 oz) silken tofu

50 g (2 oz) caster sugar

1 egg white

crème fraîche or natural yogurt,
   to serve

cocoa powder, for dusting

AWARENESS POINTS

- Green cardamom is one of the most expensive spices weight for weight so treat it as a delicacy – handle with care, especially when you release the seeds.
- Appreciate its unique smell. Can you detect the smoky tones?
- When you swallow, notice how the cardamom flavour jumps out of the creamy sweetness.

Put the chocolate and milk in a heatproof bowl and melt over a saucepan of gently simmering water.

To release the cardamom seeds, crush the pods using a pestle and mortar. Discard the pods and crush the seeds finely.

Place the cardamom pods and tofu in a food processor with half of the sugar and blend well to a smooth paste. Turn the mixture into a large bowl.

Whisk the egg white in a thoroughly clean bowl until it forms peaks. Gradually whisk in the remaining sugar.

Beat the melted chocolate mixture into the tofu until completely combined. Using a large metal spoon, fold in the egg white. Spoon the mousse into small coffee cups or glasses and chill for at least 1 hour. Serve topped with spoonfuls of crème fraîche or yogurt and a light dusting of cocoa powder.

Lemon, pistachio & date squares

Calories per square 174 (not including optional chocolate coating)

Makes 15–20

Preparation time 10 minutes, plus cooling and chilling

Cooking time 20 minutes

grated rind of 1 lemon

75 g (3 oz) ready-to-eat dried dates, chopped

75 g (3 oz) unsalted pistachios, chopped

75 g (3 oz) flaked almonds, chopped

125 g (4 oz) soft light brown sugar

150 g (5 oz) millet flakes

40 g (1½ oz) cornflakes, lightly crushed

400 g (13 oz) can condensed milk

25 g (1 oz) mixed seeds, such as pumpkin and sunflower

Simply place all the ingredients in a large bowl and mix together. Spoon into a 28 x 18 cm (11 x 7 inch) baking tin and bake in a preheated oven, 180°C (350°F), Gas Mark 4, for 20 minutes.

Remove from the oven and leave to cool, then mark into 15–20 squares and chill until firm. If you fancy, you could drizzle the top with some melted chocolate once the squares are cooled.

For chocolate & almond squares, make the mixture as above, omitting the pistachios and flaked almonds. Roughly chop 100 g (3½ oz) blanched almonds and add to the mixture with 65 g (2½ oz) bran flakes and 50 (2 oz) melted plain chocolate. Cook and cool, mark and chill as above, drizzling the top with melted white chocolate once cooled, if liked.

AWARENESS POINTS

- Close your eyes, take a pinch from the bowl mixture and see if you can identify which fruits, seeds or nut you are eating.
- Can you make out the lemon in the final bake? How does it complement the rich nutty flavour?
- Batch cook these so they can be served to friends, given out at work or enjoyed as a healthy lunchbox treat.

Guided practice

Puddings are often associated with comfort and warmth. Before you start this recipe, read the text at the start of the chapter and see what food triggers you notice. What has led up to cooking this recipe? Is there an emotional need for soothing? Did a particular memory or thought come to mind? Be kind to yourself, welcome and accept any thoughts as they come to pass.

1 This nourishing pudding is full of taste – cream and butter should be used in moderation, and healthier options used if you prefer. Try to think of it as part of a balanced diet, rather than a guilty pleasure or a reward.

2 Take the time to find different cherries depending on what is in season and available in your supermarket – canned or fresh, you should be able to get an array of colours and sweetness. Before you add the vanilla pod, rub it slightly between your hands and smell the rich aroma. Does the smell of peel and cloves make you feel wintery?

3 As you layer up the pudding to serve, make sure you appreciate all the intricate flavours that have gone in to this dish. Each layer, from the crumble to the cream, should have its own distinct rich taste – distinguish each one with your eye on the spoon; don't just shovel and gulp in one big mush.

4 How does the warmth of the crumble combine with the soothing cool cream? Does the cinnamon bring out a tart flavour in the cherries? Has the fruit juice softened the biscuit crumble? Can you make out the sharp fizz of the orange peel?

Cherries with cinnamon crumble

Calories per serving 440
Serves 4–6
Preparation time 15 minutes, plus cooling
Cooking time 20 minutes

1.5 kg (3 lb) cherries, pitted
250 g (8 oz) caster sugar
400 ml (14 fl oz) water
1 vanilla pod
2 cloves
strips of orange peel

Crumble
60 g (2¼ oz) fruit loaf
15 g (¼ oz) unsalted butter
1/8 teaspoon ground cinnamon
1 tablespoon caster sugar

Cinnamon cream
1 tablespoon icing sugar
150 ml (¼ pint) whipping cream
¼ teaspoon ground cinnamon

Put the cherries in a large bowl. Place the sugar in a heavy-based saucepan and add the measurement water, vanilla pod, cloves and orange peel. Bring to the boil, stirring occasionally, then pour the syrup over the cherries. Leave to cool.

Make the crumble. Cut the fruit loaf into 1 cm (½ inch) dice. Melt the butter and drizzle it over the fruit loaf. Mix together the cinnamon and sugar and sprinkle over the fruit loaf. Mix well, transfer to a baking sheet and cook in a preheated oven, 190°C (375°F), Gas Mark 5, for 4–5 minutes until golden and crunchy. Leave to cool.

Meanwhile, make the cinnamon cream. Sift the icing sugar over the cream, add the cinnamon and whisk until firm peaks form.

Serve the cherries with a small amount of syrup, a spoonful of the cinnamon cream and a sprinkling of the fruit loaf crumble. Decorate with the strips of orange peel.

Moist banana & carrot cake

Calories per serving 183

Serves 14 slices

Preparation time 10 minutes, plus cooling

Cooking time 1 hour 40 minutes

butter, for greasing
175 g (6 oz) ready-to-eat dried apricots, roughly chopped
125 ml (4 fl oz) water
1 egg
2 tablespoons clear honey
100 g (3½ oz) walnuts, roughly chopped
500 g (1 lb) ripe bananas, mashed
1 large carrot, about 125 g (4 oz), grated
225 g (7½ oz) self-raising flour, sifted

Topping
150 g (5 oz) cream cheese
2 tablespoons lemon curd

AWARENESS POINTS

- Shop around for different types of honey – you'll find a huge range of flavours.
- Take the time to appreciate how amazing the natural process of bees making honey is.
- What flavour is strongest – the apricot, the banana or the lemon? Would you adjust the recipe next time?

Grease a 1 kg (2 lb) loaf tin and line with nonstick baking paper. Place the apricots in a small saucepan with the measurement water, bring to the boil and simmer for 10 minutes. Transfer to a blender or food processor and blend to a thick purée.

Put all the other cake ingredients in a large bowl and add the apricot purée. Mix well, then spoon into the prepared tin.

Bake in a preheated oven, 180°C (350°F), Gas Mark 4, for 1½ hours or until a skewer inserted in the centre comes out clean. Turn out on to a wire rack to cool.

Beat together the cream cheese and lemon curd and spread over the top of the loaf.

Chocolate sorbet

Calories per serving 295

Serves 6–8

Makes about 900 ml (1½ pints)

Preparation time 15 minutes,
   plus chilling and freezing

Cooking time 10 minutes

600 ml (1 pint) water

150 g (5 oz) soft dark brown sugar

200 g (7 oz) granulated sugar

65 g (2½ oz) unsweetened cocoa powder

25 g (1 oz) plain dark chocolate with
   70% cocoa solids, finely chopped

2½ teaspoons vanilla extract

1 teaspoon instant espresso
   coffee powder

Put the measurement water, sugars and cocoa powder in a saucepan and mix together. Heat gently, stirring until the sugar has dissolved. Increase the heat to bring the mixture to a boil, then reduce to a simmer for 8 minutes.

Remove the pan from the heat and stir in the chocolate, vanilla extract and espresso powder until thoroughly dissolved. Pour into a bowl and cool over ice or leave to cool and chill.

Freeze in an ice-cream machine according to the manufacturer's instructions. Serve immediately or transfer to a chilled plastic freezerproof container and store in the freezer for up to 1 month. If you are using the sorbet straight from the freezer, transfer to the refrigerator 20 minutes before serving to soften slightly.

AWARENESS POINTS

- See if you can learn to love the natural taste of unsweetened chocolate.

- Does the espresso smell trigger anything? Does it make you feel enlivened?

- Add a small scoop of sorbet to different fresh fruit throughout the week for a healthy treat.

Ricotta & maple syrup cheesecake

Calories per serving 375

Serves 8

Preparation time 20 minutes,
   plus chilling

3 gelatine leaves

125 g (4 oz) digestive biscuits, crushed

50 g (2 oz) reduced-fat sunflower
   spread, melted

200 g (7 oz) cottage cheese

200 g (7 oz) ricotta cheese

2 egg whites

25 g (1 oz) icing sugar, sieved

25 ml (1 fl oz) lemon juice

50 ml (2 fl oz) water

4 tablespoons maple syrup

To decorate

2 oranges, peeled and sliced

sprigs of redcurrants

Line a 20 cm (8 inch) springform tin with nonstick baking paper. Soften the gelatine in cold water.

Mix together the biscuit crumbs and melted sunflower spread and press into the prepared tin. Refrigerate.

Sieve together the cottage cheese and ricotta. Whisk the egg whites in a thoroughly clean bowl until stiffly peaking, then beat in the icing sugar until glossy.

Put the lemon juice and measurement water in a saucepan over a low heat and stir in the gelatine until dissolved. Add to the ricotta mix with the maple syrup, then fold in the egg whites. Pour the mixture over the biscuit base and refrigerate until set.

Decorate with the sliced oranges and sprigs of redcurrants before serving.

AWARENESS POINTS

- If you like to know the science behind what you are cooking, then this is a recipe for you. There are plenty of ingredients that change from solid to liquid state and vice versa in this method – maybe do some reading to discover why.
- Watch the gelatine soften – what do you know about its molecular structure?
- Enjoy the feel of the biscuit crumbling between your fingers – don't be afraid to get messy. Think about the surface area of the breadcrumbs.

The one-month eating plan

Kindly remember that this is an invitation to relearn the joy of eating well and giving up an unnecessary struggle.

Week one:

- **Five days (or more)** start a mindful eating practice as explained on page 19. Initially it might be best to choose a short meal to eat on your own.

- **Use a notebook** and write down what you felt when eating mindfully.

- **Ask yourself:**
  Am I really hungry? Starving/ hungry/ slightly hungry/ not really hungry?
  Is my portion size appropriate for my hunger? Yes/No?
  Is it food I really want or other forms of nourishment, e.g. relaxation?

- **Five days a week** practice the Body Scan exercise (see page 14).

- At least **five times a week** engage in an everyday informal mindfulness practice (e.g. mindful shower, mindful tooth brushing, etc.)

Week two:

- **Continue with a mindful eating practice** (as in week one) five times a week – now try a main meal even if you only manage three spoonfuls. Again use your notebook as before.

- **Do a mindful movement practice** (e.g. mindful walking, mindful swimming) five times a week

- **Two days a week practice** the Body Scan exercise (see page 14).

Week three:

- **Continue with a mindful eating practice** (as in week one) five times a week – now try a main meal with others (see page 88). Again use your notebook as before.

- **Exercise:** Do the breath awareness practice for 5-10 minutes (see pages 32–3). Do a mindful movement practice (e.g. mindful walking, mindful swimming) five times a week

- **Two days a week** practice the Body Scan exercise (see page 14).

Week four:

- **Continue with a mindful eating practice** (as in week one) five times a week. Also focus on 'finding your triggers' (see pages 22–30). Again use your notebook as before.

- **Do a mindful movement** practice five times a week.

- **Alternate Body Scan** or a breath exercise five times a week.

- **Try something new every day...**

And now ...

Do a selection from the above for the rest of your life.

Weekly eating planner

This meal plan offers a few suggestions of what to eat for the first week of eating mindfully. For the following weeks, try to listen to your body's signals and choose your own recipes accordingly.

Monday

BREAKFAST: Very berry fromage frais fool | PAGE 52

LUNCH: Chicken minestrone | PAGE 67

DINNER: Lentil moussaka | PAGE 107

Tuesday

BREAKFAST: Granola squares | PAGE 55

LUNCH: Beetroot, spinach & orange salad | PAGE 74

DINNER: Burmese chicken noodle curry | PAGE 114

Wednesday

BREAKFAST: Porridge with prune compote | PAGE 41

LUNCH: Aromatic chicken parcels | PAGE 76

DINNER: Seafood & vegetable stir fry | PAGE 112

Thursday

BREAKFAST: Figs with honey & yoghurt | PAGE 58

LUNCH: Greek country salad with haloumi | PAGE 78

DINNER: Salmon curry with tomato salad | PAGE 106

Friday

BREAKFAST: Cranberry muffins | PAGE 43

LUNCH: Seared chicken sandwich | PAGE 80

DINNER: Quick prosciutto & rocket pizza | PAGE 94

Saturday

BREAKFAST: Moroccan baked eggs | PAGE 49

LUNCH: Salmon and bulghar wheat | PAGE 63

DINNER: Lamb stuffed with rice & peppers | PAGE 89

Sunday

BREAKFAST: Banana & sultana drop scones | PAGE 47

LUNCH: Roast pork & fennel | PAGE 95

DINNER: Squash, kale & mixed bean soup | PAGE 105

Index

Acknowledgements

The Mindfulness Cookbook Picture Acknowledgements

Recipe photography © Octopus Publishing Group

Additional photography:
Alamy moodboard 116; PhotoAlto sas 12. Getty Images Fuse 84; Guido Mieth 58;
  Joshua Hodge Photography 28; Michael H 8; Ryan McVay 36; T-Pool/STOCK4B 30.